Sheila G's

butter&chocolate

To all the chocoholics, brownie lovers, dessert fanatics—
you know who you are.

*You also know that dessert is not just something to eat after a meal, it's something
to savor and share. It adds a special sweetness to life. And I bet you enjoy, as I do,
the tremendous amount of satisfaction that comes from making something with
your own two hands, and seeing it put a smile on someone else's face.*
I'm so blessed to be able to do what I love!

Sheila G's

butter & chocolate

101 creative sweets
and treats using
brownie batter

Sheila G. Mains

KYLE BOOKS

Published in 2016 by Kyle Books
www.kylebooks.com

Distributed by National Book Network
4501 Forbes Blvd., Suite 200,
Lanham, MD 20706
Phone: (800) 462-6420
Fax: (800) 338-4550
CustomerCare@nbnbooks.com

10 9 8 7 6 5 4 3 2 1

ISBN 978-1-909487-51-2

Project Editor: Jessica Goodman
Copy Editor: Sarah Scheffel
Designer: Alison Lew, Vertigo Design NYC
Photographer: Tina Rupp
Food Stylist: Lisa Homa
Prop Stylist: Karin Olsen
Production: Nic Jones, Gemma John, and Lisa Pinnell

Library of Congress Control Number: 2016935537

Color reproduction by f1 colour
Printed and bound in China by C&C Offset Printing Co., Ltd.

contents

batter, brownies & brittle, oh my!

Memories of childhood and chocolate

My mother, Hilda, worked full-time, even when my sister Judi and I were growing up. Yet she somehow managed to put a meal on the table every night. Every night, that is, except Friday. That's when my father took the whole family out to eat.

So here's how she did it: Every Sunday, my grandmother Rose came to our house, and together they prepared meals for the week ahead. Baking was a significant part of this weekly cook-off. My grandmother's specialty was rugelach—a bite-size pastry made with a buttery yeast dough filled with cinnamon and golden raisins. My mother's was Congo bars.

Congo bars were essentially flour, eggs, and brown sugar—similar to what's now referred to as a blonde brownie. What made my mom's Congo bars so spectacular—and hooked me on chocolate f-o-r-e-v-e-r—was that she sprinkled the chocolate chips

on top instead of mixing them in the batter. Then when she removed the pan from the oven, she'd take a spatula and smear the chocolate from side to side and corner to corner. Looking back, I realize just how smart my mom was: Making a pan of bars was way faster than making cookies—and every bit as tasty.

My mother never said, "C'mon, I'll teach you how to cook." I learned by observing her and my grandmother all those Sundays. There was nowhere I'd rather have been than in the kitchen with them. I watched as they created main courses, sides, and desserts, using whatever was in the fridge, pantry, and cupboards. I saw how a few basic recipes became the building blocks for a wide variety of dishes and desserts. And I discovered that cooking—especially baking—is just as creative as painting a masterpiece.

MAKE EVERY BITE WORTH IT

Their philosophy—and mine as well—was if you're going to go to the effort of making something from scratch, use the very best ingredients. Nothing low-fat, sugar-free, preservative-laden. No skimping. No shortcuts. (Okay, sometimes you can take a shortcut as long as it doesn't affect the quality.)

I say if you're going to indulge, go for broke. After all, it's not something you do every day, right? Once you come around to this way of thinking, you're less likely to pick up just anything to satisfy your sweet tooth. The recipes in this cookbook subscribe to this "butter is better" approach; and, as luck would have it, are in step with today's cooking trends.

I still have my grandmother's original, handwritten brownie recipe, which is the basis for my Signature Brownies, along with my mom's Congo bar recipe on a tattered, chocolate-stained piece of paper. What a legacy they left me.

DO WHAT YOU LOVE

I always thought my dad, who was an auto mechanic his entire life, was the most successful person I knew. That's because there was a spring in his step every day as he left for work. He absolutely loved what he did for a living. His advice to me: Do what you love, no matter what. Somewhere along the way, that message was lost on me.

I enrolled in business school and held several accounting jobs over the years. It paid the bills, but I didn't love it—especially during tax season. What I loved was baking. In fact, I would whip up a cheesecake in a New York minute if someone at the office was celebrating a birthday. Invite me to your party, and I'd show up with a platter of cookie dough brownies or white chocolate-cherry macadamia nut bars. I was never happier than when I was sharing some sweet thing I made.

My friends encouraged me to trade bean counting for baking. *Gee, Sheila, these brownies are so yummy you should quit your job and bake full-time.* That's when I began to question what I was doing. Was accounting really what I wanted to do for the rest of my life? No! I'd rather be baking. (And since "cooking the books" is against the law that was out!) But could I make a career—and a living—armed with a spatula and an oven? How much dough (the green kind) did I need to get started?

And what would it be like to be my own boss, and control my own destiny?

A GIANT LEAP OF FAITH

It turns out, the decision wasn't mine to make. I was laid off from my CFO position at an industrial advertising agency in November 1992. I chose to look at this as my now-or-never opportunity. I decided to take the advice of family and friends and give baking a whirl. I came up with the catchy name "Brownie Points" and started delivering platters of my Signature Brownies to local hotels and restaurants. Managers and chefs alike raved about the product and the presentation, but when they discovered I wasn't a licensed commercial baker, they showed me the door.

So, in April 1993, I took a giant leap of faith and leased a 1,200-square-foot facility, purchased equipment at auctions, passed inspections, and obtained my license. I was a full-fledged baker. A Realtor friend started ordering tins of brownies to give to his buyers and sellers. It seemed everyone who received a tin became a customer. Word of mouth was building. Just about then, the toll-free number 1-800-BROWNIE became available. I grabbed it.

Two years later, I knew my hard work was finally going to pay off. The Executive Chef of EPCOT at Disney World called my brownie "hotline." He'd sampled my brownies and liked them! Next came a purchase order for 37,000 brownies! Once I caught my breath, I did a little victory dance around my giant commercial mixer. To this day, Disney is still a customer.

ROLLER COASTER RIDE

The next twenty years were jam-packed with ups and downs, successes and setbacks. I lived and breathed brownies. As demand increased, I turned the day-to-day baking over to larger and larger commercial bakers. Through it all, I recognized two common threads: Everyone loved the crispy edges of my brownies, and everyone fought over the corner pieces.

As I walked through the bakery, day after day, picking the brittle brownie batter off the sides of the sheet pans as the brownies cooled, I kept thinking, Wouldn't it be great if I could figure out a way to make whole pans of crunchy edges?

In 2010, after many starts and stops, I launched BROWNIE BRITTLE™—a sweet snack made of thin pieces of brownie batter with a delightfully satisfying crunch. My desire to create an entirely new experience for all the brownie lovers out there turned into a multimillion-dollar business. (You'll even find several recipes in *Sheila G's Butter & Chocolate* that incorporate BROWNIE BRITTLE™ as an ingredient.)

FROM SCRATCH, YET OH-SO-SIMPLE

For many of those early years, I was a single, working mom, and the memory of how frantic those years were is just one of the reasons I decided to write this cookbook. It was during that period when time and money were in short supply that I'd scout out every restaurant in South Florida looking for "kids eat free" nights. Mondays were Taco Bell; Tuesdays, Mickey D's; Wednesdays, the neighborhood pizza joint. I would cook, but unlike my mother, it was one or two nights at best—and usually only on weekends.

For me, this cookbook is for all the parents, grandparents, and singles out there who throw a box of doughnuts from the supermarket bakery into their shopping cart because they think they don't have time to bake. These simple, from-scratch recipes prove otherwise.

I also wanted to share my recipes so others can experience the joy of watching family and friends eat every last crumb of the desserts they make. People may race through their meals, but they linger over dessert. The recipes here provide the sweetest way to connect.

MY COMFORT ZONE

A friend sent me a greeting card a while back that said: "Stressed is desserts spelled backwards. Coincidence? I think not!" That was not the first time I'd heard that, but on that particular day, it really struck a chord. I realized my response to stress was to whip up something warm and chocolatey. Baking was my de-stressor. The kitchen was my comfort zone.

Okay, I'm aware there are bakers who embrace complicated recipes. I'm not one of them! I'm not interested in a dessert that has twenty ingredients and sixteen steps. I'm all for quick and easy—as long as it's still delicious. That's why just about every sweet treat in this book springs from three or four recipes and uses staples found in almost every kitchen.

Now, before you yawn and say, "Well, that certainly sounds boring," remember: once you've got these recipes down pat, you can get creative. Stick raw edible cookie dough in the center of that mini muffin. Experiment with different-shaped pans. Make cookies, bars, truffles, or ice cream sandwiches using these simple, basic recipes as your starting point.

You'll be oh-so-glad to have them in your repertoire the next time you're invited to a potluck dinner at the last minute, or your child tells you at 9 p.m. that you're the dessert mommy at school the next day.

FROM MY HEART TO YOURS

Practically every civilization uses a phrase similar to "hearth and home." That's because every mud hut, log cabin, teepee, and castle had a hearth—an open fireplace that provided warmth, light, and most important, a place to prepare food for family and friends. When I look at "hearth," I see the word "heart." And isn't that what kitchens are today—the very heart of our homes?

I hope the sweets and treats in this cookbook warm the hearts of your family and friends, and inspire you to create your own butter and chocolate masterpieces.

enjoy!

xoxo,
Sheila

equipment

EVERYDAY UTENSILS AND TOOLS

By design, almost every recipe in this cookbook uses baking pans, utensils, and tools found in most kitchens. Here's a brief inventory of everyday essentials you'll need to make the 101 recipes in this cookbook:

Baking pans—8 × 8-inch and 9 × 13-inch
Baking sheets
Bowls for mixing, melting, and storage
Cookie cutters
Hand mixer
Measuring cups and spoons
Microwave oven
Mini muffin pans
Pie pan, 9-inch
Saucepans
Sharp paring knife
Small sieve for dusting confectioners' sugar
Spatulas
Wire racks for cooling

Since many of my recipes require melting butter, chocolate, and other ingredients in a microwave, I suggest you have several microwave-safe bowls of various sizes on hand. I prefer glass, but Styrene-free plastic works as well.

Now, let's talk about some of the gadgets and gizmos out there that are not necessary, but sure make baking easier and more fun. Plus, they definitely raise your dessert's WOW factor.

CAKE POP MAKER

If these lollipop cakes are popular at your house, you might want to invest in a cake pop maker. Most models make twelve at a time and retail for as low as eighteen dollars. If you don't want even one more appliance in your kitchen, no matter how compact it is, you can make your cake pops using an electric mixer or food processor, and roll them by hand.

For serving, I've been known to stick my cake pops in foam blocks or tall glasses. However, if you really want to show off your creations, purchase a reusable, tiered cake pop stand. And remember to pick up some pop sticks. Sure, you could eat these with a fork, but half the fun of a cake pop is twirling one around in your mouth. Pop sticks usually come fifty to a bag and range in size from three to eight inches.

CHOCOLATE DIPPING TOOLS

Chocolate dipping tools—two- or three-tined forks, swirls, and baskets—make dipping and enrobing desserts in chocolate so much easier. Find them online or at restaurant and kitchen supply stores.

CULINARY TORCH

Along with caramelizing sugar and browning meringue, you also can use a culinary torch to sear tomato skins, melt cheese on soup, and toast breadcrumbs. There are many videos on YouTube that demonstrate how to use one.

DOUGHNUT AND DOUGHNUT HOLE PANS

My mother used to make doughnuts by rolling the dough into balls and then dropping two or three at a time into hot oil. They were yummy, but labor intensive. Plus, they had to be placed on paper towels to absorb some of the grease.

Today, there are special pans to make doughnut holes and doughnuts. The typical capacity for a doughnut pan is six, with each cavity having a raised center to create the doughnut hole; doughnut hole pans have twelve to twenty cavities.

JELLYROLL PAN

Jellyroll pans differ from standard baking or flat cookie sheets because their sides are one-inch deep, making it easier to handle cake dough and prevent it from spilling off the pan. These pans were originally designed for baking cake rolls or jellyrolls, but have many other practical applications. If you don't have a jellyroll pan, you can use a baking sheet with sides.

LOOSE-BOTTOM OR SPRINGFORM PAN

If you only make cheesecake once in a while, a springform pan is fine, but I've replaced my springform pans so many times over the years, it finally made sense to invest in a sturdy, loose-bottom pan. With a loose-bottom pan, the bottom rests on a small rim and can be pushed up from the bottom of the pan. You still might need to loosen the cake from the sides of the pan with a knife or thin spatula as it cools. Then, just hold one side of the pan and push up from the bottom.

A springform is a two-piece pan that has a round base and a two- to three-inch high interlocking band that opens and closes with the flip of a latch. Both are ideal for tarts and cheesecakes. My recipes call for a 9-inch pan.

MADELEINE PAN

The only way to create the French butter cake known as a "madeleine" is with this particular pan. Each madeleine pan has twelve shell-shaped cups that give the classic cake its scalloped and ribbed appearance.

OFFSET SPATULA

An offset spatula is a versatile baking tool shaped like a putty knife, super for spreading frosting. The angled blade elevates your hand and helps keep fingers and sleeves out of the way.

PASTRY BLADE

This stainless steel blade is what I use to remove brownies from the pan. It's sharp and some even feature 1-inch markings for precise measuring. It's also ideal for cutting dough and sectioning pie crusts.

PASTRY OR PIPING BAG AND TIPS

Cone- or triangular-shaped and made from cloth, paper, or plastic, this handy dandy tool is my favorite way to perk up and personalize desserts. All you have to do is fill the bag at the wide end and squeeze the contents through the narrow opening at the other end.

Use a rounded tip to pipe whipped cream, jelly, custard, or brownie filling into doughnuts, pastries, and fruit. Nozzles shaped like stars, leaves, and flowers make decorating cakes, pies, and muffins a breeze.

SCOOPS

When measuring out batter, my favorite tool is a scoop. The ones I have in my kitchen are stainless steel and have spring-loaded handles that slide a band across the bottom of the scoop to release batter in a round shape. They're more accurate, less messy, and faster than your everyday spoon. The recipes in this cookbook use the following scoop capacities:

Small: 1¼ inch = 2 teaspoons
Medium: 1½ inch = 1 tablespoon
Large: 2¼ inch = ¼ cup

TRIFLE BOWL

While any bowl that's seven or more inches deep and wide at the top will do, a clear glass bowl with a pedestal is the best way to show off a trifle. And you will want to show it off. This gloriously colorful, layered dessert is a work of art that deserves to take center stage.

WAFFLE CONE MAKER

When I was a kid, everyone had a waffle iron. My mom said she and dad received three as wedding gifts. It seems no self-respecting homemaker was without a waffle maker—or two. Today, there are waffle cone makers that come with a cone shaper enabling you to make cones out of real waffles.

pantry

Most of the ingredients in this cookbook are in all probability already in your fridge, cupboards, and spice rack, except for a few specialty items. If you're a chocoholic like I am, you're probably covered in that department as well.

Here's a partial list of ingredients found in *Sheila G's Butter & Chocolate* along with a few baking tips and a little lore.

BAKING COCOA

Baking cocoa is a powder made from cacao beans. It has no fat and is never sweetened. The intense, deep chocolate taste that is a result of removing most of the cocoa butter is ideal for desserts and frostings where the goal is rich, fudgy flavor. Semisweet chocolate chips and baking cocoa are what give my Signature Brownies such a high chocolate profile. Look on the label to be sure the brand you choose is 100 percent baking cocoa.

BROWNIE BRITTLE™

BROWNIE BRITTLE™, the award-winning sweet snack sensation I created, is my claim to fame. It comes in five flavors: Chocolate Chip, Salted Caramel, Mint Chocolate Chip, Toffee Crunch, and Peanut Butter Chip. Any of the flavors work to create crunchy, chocolatey crusts and toppings in the bar, pie, and cheesecake recipes found herein. However, the original Chocolate Chip seems to go best with everything. BROWNIE BRITTLE™, which can best be described as thin pieces of baked brownie batter, is available in 1-, 2-, 2.75, 5-, 14-, 16-, and 20-ounce bags, and can be found in tens of thousands of stores nationwide and online at BrownieBrittle.com. Can't find BROWNIE BRITTLE™? Substitute store-bought chocolate wafers in the recipes that call for BROWNIE BRITTLE™.

BUTTER

Butter usually contains about 80 percent fat. The higher the fat content the richer, more flavorful the dessert. Butter is made from fresh cream, and comes unsalted and salted. The majority of the recipes in this cookbook use salted sweet cream butter, which, I realize, is a departure from most baked goods recipes. I have no other reason than that is what I buy for home use. Feel free to substitute unsalted butter if that is what you have on hand; it will not affect the taste or texture. Butter is a real palate-pleaser and contributes immensely to the moistness and superior mouthfeel of baked sweets and treats.

CHOCOLATE

These days we don't have to settle for just semisweet chocolate chips. We're fortunate enough to be able to purchase bags of these miniature morsels in milk, semisweet, dark, bittersweet, and white chocolate.

The darker the chocolate, the lower the sugar content—and the higher the percentage of cocoa. To me, semisweet and bittersweet chips are ideal for baking because they deliver a rich chocolate taste without being too sweet, and they hold their shape so well in cookies, muffins, and cakes. While both are about 75 percent cocoa, bittersweet chocolate has a hint of vanilla and more of the chocolate liquor that comes from pressing the cocoa beans.

Milk chocolate chips are 20 percent cocoa and have a high percentage of milk powder added, which means they melt quickly. So if you prefer sweeter, gooey treats, milk chocolate chips are for you.

Then, of course, there's white chocolate, which really isn't chocolate at all, because it contains no cocoa solids. Instead it's made from cocoa butter, milk, and vanilla. But, you can't dismiss the sweet creaminess, unique flavor, and striking contrast it brings to whatever dessert is lucky enough to have white chocolate in it—or on it.

DAIRY

All my recipes call for whole (not 2 percent, low-fat, or skim) milk, cream, and cheese products and large, premium eggs. Remember, if you're going to indulge in dessert, then indulge. We've already talked about butter. So here is an inventory of the other dairy products used in this cookbook.

> Buttermilk
> Condensed milk
> Cream: light, heavy, whipping
> Cream cheese
> Eggs
> Half-and-half
> Milk: almond, low-fat, whole
> Ricotta cheese

DULCE DE LECHE

In Spanish, "dulce" means sweet or candy and "leche" means milk. This "milk candy" or "sweet milk" is similar to caramel. The difference is that dulce de leche is mostly milk with a little sugar, whereas, caramel is simply sugar that's been heated. Both are similar in color; however, caramel is stickier. Dulce de leche is smooth and creamy with a soft flavor.

Different stores have various ideas about where to stock dulce de leche. I've found it in these three places: the baking aisle; in with the coffee and tea next to cans of evaporated and condensed milk; and in the ethnic aisle near the Hispanic products.

There are recipes online for making dulce de leche from scratch, but the canned version is so exceptional—and so easy—it is one of those shortcuts I choose to take.

FRUIT

With a few exceptions, the recipes in this cookbook use fruit as garnish. Follow my suggestions as to which ones pair well with certain recipes, or serve those favorites that appeal to your family and friends. Remember, fresh matters. So always choose fruit in season. That's when prices are lowest, and taste, color, and texture are at their peak.

FUN STUFF

How can funky ingredients like fluff, gummy worms, and sprinkles not make you smile? These novelties add a whimsical dimension to many of the butter and chocolate basics in this cookbook. Some help recreate popular candy bars while others turn ordinary pies and tarts into creative masterpieces. When you're looking for a treat to surprise—and delight—guests of every age, choose an ingredient from this list, match it to a recipe, and get ready to have some fun.

> Candy corn
> Fudge sauce
> Gummy worms
> Ice cream
> Maraschino cherries
> Marshmallow fluff
> Peppermint candy sticks
> Pretzels
> Pudding
> Sprinkles
> Toffee bits
> Whipped topping

NUTS

Nuts add crunchiness and extra flavor, especially when toasted, to desserts. If you live near a fresh market or a Costco, buy your nuts in bulk and chop them as you need them. (They'll last for months in airtight packaging in the freezer.) Your next best option is to pick up nuts from the supermarket when you're ready to bake. Here are my faves:

Almonds
Dry roasted peanuts
Hazelnuts
Macadamia nuts
Pecans
Pistachios
Walnuts

PEANUT BUTTER

All-natural peanut butter should have one ingredient: peanuts! There are several national brands that offer what I call "real" peanut butter. Check your local supermarket. Many stores grind peanuts on the premises and stock this all-natural staple in the deli section. Peanut oil rises to the top, so be sure to mix thoroughly before adding to any recipe.

SANDING SUGAR

Sanding sugar is coarsely ground white sugar. Choose from a variety of colors, or purchase it plain and color it yourself. Because of its large crystals, sanding sugar doesn't melt during baking, and is a fun way to add a little crunch and color to baked goods. Look for it in the baking aisle of your supermarket or in specialty baking shops.

SEA SALT

So what's the big deal about sea salt? Well, it has three things going for it: taste, texture, and minimal processing. Sea salt, which is the result of the evaporation of ocean water or water from saltwater lakes, undergoes very little processing. Consequently, minerals are left in giving it a different flavor and color,

and a coarser texture and irregular shapes. I always use coarse sea salt.

Table salt, on the other hand, comes from underground salt deposits, and is more heavily refined. Minerals are stripped out, and iodine and additives to prevent clumping are put in. However, there's very little difference in nutritional value and the amount of sodium by weight between sea and table salt. I must admit sprinkling sea salt on chocolate, caramel, or practically anything sweet sparks a whole new flavor sensation.

SPICES, ETC.

Whenever possible, use pure almond, peppermint, and vanilla extracts. They may cost a little more than imitation flavorings, but are worth it. They are made from oils and other natural ingredients, and deliver a more concentrated flavor essence. They are the best choice for baking. Also, choose ground spices. They produce the zingiest flavor. If your spices have lost their fragrance, then the taste is gone as well. Replace them. These are the spices, seasonings, colors, and flavorings that put the pep in my recipes:

Allspice
Almond extract
Cinnamon
Cloves
Dry yeast
Egg replacer
Espresso powder
Evaporated milk
Gelatin
Ginger
Instant coffee
Nutmeg
Peppermint extract
Red food coloring
Salt
Sea salt
Vanilla bean
Vanilla extract
Vinegar

SPIRITS

I've included a handful of recipes—Bacon and Bourbon Brownies and Blonde Amaretto Truffles, for example—with a bit of a kick to them. Not enough to make you tipsy—just enough to enhance flavor and moistness. While baking does burn off some of the alcohol, there's enough left over to lift your spirits. Cheers!

> Amaretto
> Baileys® Irish Cream
> Bourbon
> Grand Marnier®
> Kahlúa®
> Original Moonshine® Corn Whiskey
> Rum: light & dark

SUGAR AND OTHER SWEET THINGS

The most common sugar used in baking is granulated sugar, also called refined, table, or white sugar. It is processed from beets or sugarcane that has been crystallized and then dried.

Brown sugar is refined white sugar with molasses added to it, which gives it its brown color and rich flavor. The only difference between light and dark brown sugar is the molasses content.

Confectioners' sugar, also known as powdered or icing sugar, is granulated sugar that has been ground into a fine powder. The 10X on the box signifies that the granulated sugar has been ground ten times to achieve such fineness. Confectioners' sugar is most often used in frostings and in recipes where a light dusting is the perfect finishing touch.

Here's how to measure sugar: Granulated or confectioner's sugar should be spooned into a dry measuring cup and leveled off. Brown sugar should be packed firmly into a dry measure so it holds its shape when turned out.

Other ingredients that lend their sweetness to my recipes include:

> Agave
> Butterscotch chips
> Caramels
> Chocolate wafers
> Corn syrup, light
> Honey
> Jelly and preserves
> Maple syrup

brownie & blondie favorites

If you're a chocolate aficionado in general and a brownie enthusiast in particular, start here. This chapter introduces you to my Signature Brownie recipe—the jumping-off point for everything from Salted Caramel Brownies and Blondies to Bacon and Bourbon Brownies. There are Peanut Butter and Jelly Brownies for the young and young-at-heart crowd, as well as gluten-free and vegan options. I encourage you to try them all, and then dream up a few of your own.

signature brownies

YIELD 9 brownies

PREP 10 minutes

BAKE 30 minutes

INGREDIENTS FOR 8 × 8-INCH PAN

2 cups (12 ounces) semisweet chocolate chips

6 tablespoons salted butter

2 large eggs

1 teaspoon pure vanilla extract

½ cup sugar

½ cup all-purpose flour

½ teaspoon baking powder

¼ teaspoon salt

1 tablespoon 100% baking cocoa

YIELD 24 brownies

PREP 10 minutes

BAKE 30 minutes

INGREDIENTS FOR 9 × 13-INCH PAN

3 cups (18 ounces) semisweet chocolate chips

9 tablespoons (1 stick plus 1 tablespoon) salted butter

3 large eggs

1½ teaspoons pure vanilla extract

¾ cup sugar

¾ cup all-purpose flour

¾ teaspoon baking powder

¼ teaspoon salt, heaping

1½ tablespoons 100% baking cocoa

This recipe is the one that started my love affair with chocolate in general and brownies in particular. Handed down from my grandmother Rose to my mom, Hilda, and then on to me, it is the best brownie recipe ever. Why? Because it blends two chocolates: semisweet and cocoa powder. Most brownie recipes call for one or the other, rarely both, but the double dose of chocolate delivers a much more interesting flavor profile.

My Signature Brownies are dense, chocolatey, and rich enough to stand on their own. However, if your family simply has to have frosting, whip up your favorite from scratch or try my Cream Cheese Frosting recipe on page 30. Prefer a more cakelike brownie? Simply add an extra egg to the recipe for an 8 × 8-inch pan or two extra eggs to the 9 × 13-inch recipe.

1. Preheat the oven to 350°F. Grease an 8 × 8-inch or 9 × 13-inch pan and set aside.

2. Microwave the chocolate chips and butter in a microwave-safe bowl on high for 30 seconds; remove and stir. Return to the microwave if not completely melted and microwave in 15-second intervals until smooth and creamy. (Do not overheat or the chocolate will scorch.)

3. Mix together the eggs, vanilla, and sugar in a separate bowl using an electric mixer set on the lowest speed or a spatula. Blend the egg mixture into the melted chocolate mixture until well combined.

4. Add the flour, baking powder, salt, and cocoa to the chocolate mixture and mix well by hand or using the lowest setting on the mixer.

5. Pour the batter into the prepared pan and bake for 30 minutes, until edges are crisp and the center is completely flat with a crackly surface.

6. Cool completely, and then cut into 9 squares or 24 pieces, depending on the pan size. Store in an airtight container in the refrigerator for 5 days or in the freezer for up to 6 months.

Substitute your favorite brownie box mix in any of the treats that use the Signature Brownie recipes for a 9 × 13-inch pan.

blonde brownies

YIELD 24 blondies

PREP 10 minutes

BAKE 25 to 27 minutes

12 tablespoons (1½ sticks) salted butter, melted

1½ cups light brown sugar, packed

2 large eggs

2 teaspoons pure vanilla extract

1½ cups all-purpose flour

1 teaspoon baking powder

½ teaspoon salt

What makes blonde brownies blonde? For starters, there's no cocoa in them. Instead, blondies, as they're popularly known, rely on vanilla and brown sugar for their sweetness, flavor, and golden color. Top each square with a scoop of vanilla ice cream and a drizzle of maple syrup, and you've got a real crowd-pleaser on your hands. In fact, these Blonde Brownies are my son Devin's all-time favorite.

While Devin prefers a "true" Blonde Brownie (no chips), I've been known to toss in a cup and a half of white chocolate, semisweet chocolate, or butterscotch chips occasionally. Feel free to mix and match different flavors of chips depending on your family's preference. Simply fold them into the batter once the other ingredients are thoroughly mixed.

1. Preheat the oven to 325°F. Grease a 9 × 13-inch pan and set aside.

2. Using an electric mixer or a spatula, mix together the melted butter and brown sugar until well combined. Add the eggs and vanilla and mix well. Add the flour, baking powder, and salt and mix thoroughly.

3. Spread the batter into the prepared pan and bake for 25 to 27 minutes, until toothpick inserted in center comes out clean.

4. Cool completely, and then cut into 24 squares. Store in an airtight container in the refrigerator for 5 days or in the freezer for up to 6 months.

rich chewy cocoa brownies

YIELD	9 brownies
PREP	10 minutes
BAKE	30 minutes

2 large eggs

1¾ cups sugar

2 teaspoons pure vanilla extract

12 tablespoons (1½ sticks) salted butter, melted

1¼ cups all-purpose flour

¾ cup 100% baking cocoa

½ teaspoon baking powder

¼ teaspoon salt

*B*etter than a box mix and almost as fast. One bowl. Ten-minute prep. All-natural ingredients. This recipe creates just the right butter to chocolate balance to produce a brownie that's moist and chewy inside with a crackly outside. The bittersweet baking cocoa gives these brownies their intense chocolate flavor, making them the perfect companion for vanilla-bean ice cream and a mug of freshly brewed coffee. Go ahead. Make a pan right now. You've got the time!

1. Preheat the oven to 350°F. Grease an 8 × 8-inch pan and set aside.

2. Using an electric mixer or a spatula, mix together the eggs, sugar, and vanilla until well combined. Add the melted butter and mix well. Add the flour, cocoa, baking powder, and salt and mix thoroughly.

3. Pour the batter into the prepared pan and bake for 30 minutes, until center rises and falls and edges begin to crisp.

4. Cool completely, and then cut into 9 squares.

signature vegan brownies

YIELD	9 to 12 brownies
PREP	15 minutes
BAKE	25 to 30 minutes

2 teaspoons instant coffee

5 tablespoons hot water, plus
1 tablespoon more, if needed

2 tablespoons powdered egg replacer
(found in the baking aisle in most
supermarkets)

1 cup sugar

6 tablespoons canola oil

1 teaspoon pure vanilla extract

1 cup all-purpose flour

⅔ cup 100% baking cocoa

¼ teaspoon salt

¾ cup nondairy semisweet chocolate
chips (optional)

*V*egans love brownies, too! And since I want this cookbook to inspire everyone to become master brownie bakers, I set out to create a vegan recipe that mirrored my Signature Brownies as closely as possible. Believe me when I say it took me several tries! The trick was finding replacements for eggs and dairy, among other ingredients, that would create the same mouthfeel, rich fudgy flavor, and dense texture. I'm fairly certain my grandmother Rose never heard the term "vegan," but she'd be all smiles knowing I helped dessert devotees everywhere enjoy brownies that fit their life choices.

1. Preheat the oven to 350°F. Grease an 8 × 8-inch pan with oil or nonstick cooking spray.

2. Dissolve the coffee in hot water then add egg replacer. Use a hand mixer and mix until frothy. Add the sugar and mix until blended. Add the oil and vanilla and mix well.

3. Whisk together the flour, cocoa, and salt in a separate bowl. Gradually add the dry ingredients to the wet ingredients, folding them in with a spatula or an electric mixer set on the lowest possible setting until thoroughly combined. Add up to 1 tablespoon of hot water if the batter is too stiff. Mix in nondairy chocolate chips, if desired.

4. Pour the batter into the prepared pan. Bake for 25 to 30 minutes, until toothpick inserted in center comes out clean.

5. Cool completely, and then cut into 9 to 12 pieces.

signature gluten-free brownies

YIELD	9 to 12 brownies
PREP	10 minutes
BAKE	30 minutes

*E*liminating gluten from your diet doesn't have to make you grumpy, and you don't have to sacrifice flavor and texture to feel good—especially when making my Signature Brownie recipe. All you have to do is substitute rice flour for all-purpose flour and gluten-free baking powder for regular baking powder. It's as simple as that.

2 cups (12 ounces) semisweet chocolate chips

6 tablespoons salted butter

2 large eggs

1 teaspoon pure vanilla extract

½ cup sugar

½ cup rice flour

½ teaspoon gluten-free baking powder (try Rumsford)

¼ teaspoon salt

1 tablespoon 100% baking cocoa

1. Preheat the oven to 350°F. Grease an 8 × 8-inch pan and set aside.

2. Microwave the chocolate chips and butter in a microwave-safe bowl on high for 30 seconds; remove and stir. Return to the microwave if not completely melted and microwave in 15-second intervals until smooth and creamy. (Do not overheat or the chocolate will scorch.)

3. Mix together the eggs, vanilla, and sugar in a separate bowl using an electric mixer set on the lowest speed or a spatula. Blend the egg mixture into the melted chocolate mixture until well combined. Pour the batter into the prepared pan and bake for 30 minutes, until a toothpick inserted in the center comes out clean.

4. Cool completely, and then cut into 9 or 12 pieces. Store in an airtight container in the refrigerator for 5 days or in the freezer for up to 6 months.

cookie dough brownies

YIELD   9 brownies

PREP   25 minutes

BAKE   30 minutes

BROWNIE LAYER

Signature Brownie recipe for
8 × 8 inch-pan (page 19)

COOKIE DOUGH LAYER

12 tablespoons (1½ sticks)
salted butter

¾ cup light brown sugar, packed

⅓ cup granulated sugar

1½ teaspoons pure vanilla extract

1½ cups all-purpose flour

2 tablespoons milk

CHOCOLATE TOPPING

1 cup (6 ounces) semisweet
chocolate chips

¼ teaspoon shortening or coconut oil

Every time I make this recipe, I think: The only thing missing is my grandmother smacking my hand for snacking on the raw cookie dough. With this recipe, feel free to snack away—the dough is egg-free! I'm proud to say this triple-decker brownie was the best-selling dessert at Disney World's Hollywood Studios theme park three years in a row!

1. Preheat the oven to 350°F. Grease an 8 × 8-inch pan.

2. Prepare the signature brownie batter according to directions. Bake in the prepared pan for 30 minutes, or until the center rises and falls and the edges begin to crisp. Allow to cool in the pan.

3. **PREPARE THE COOKIE DOUGH LAYER:** In a microwave-safe bowl, microwave the butter on high for 1 minute. Mix in both sugars and the vanilla using an electric mixer set on the lowest speed or a spatula. Add the flour and mix on low speed until fully blended. Add the milk and mix until the batter is moist and easy to spread. Spread the cookie dough batter on top of the cooled brownies, using a spatula to create a smooth, even layer.

4. **PREPARE THE CHOCOLATE TOPPING:** Melt the chocolate chips and shortening in a microwave-safe bowl on high for 30 seconds; remove and stir. Return to microwave if not thoroughly melted, and microwave in 15-second intervals until smooth and creamy. (Do not overheat or the chocolate will scorch.)

5. Pour the warm chocolate topping on top of the cookie dough layer and spread evenly with a spatula. Allow the topping to harden at room temperature or chill for 10 minutes to speed up the process.

6. Cut the brownies into 9 squares once the chocolate topping is set.

cream cheese brownies

YIELD	24 brownies
PREP	20 minutes
BAKE	35 to 40 minutes

Signature Brownie recipe for
9 × 13-inch pan (page 19)

1 (8-ounce) package cream cheese,
at room temperature

1 teaspoon pure vanilla extract

¼ cup sugar

1 large egg

*I*n our house, when it's your birthday, you get to plan the menu. Of course, this includes choosing the dessert. Instead of a traditional birthday cake, my stepson, Scott, always asked for a pan of these brownies.

To make them more festive, after the brownies had cooled, I always wrote "Happy Birthday" with piping gel across the top. Then, right before serving, I added birthday candles. I'm pretty sure Scott was saying "cream cheese" when we snapped his picture.

1. Preheat the oven to 350°F. Grease a 9 × 13-inch pan.

2. Prepare the signature brownie batter, pour into the prepared pan and set aside.

3. Place cream cheese in a bowl and mix with an electric mixer on medium speed for 1 minute. Mix in the vanilla, sugar, and egg, one by one. Continue to mix until ingredients are well blended.

4. Use a tablespoon to drop evenly spaced dollops of the cream cheese mixture on top of the brownie batter. Use a butter knife to swirl the cream cheese mixture into the brownie batter, leaving small areas of the brownie batter exposed to create a marbled effect.

5. Bake for 35 to 40 minutes, until top is firm and beginning to crack.

6. Cool completely, then cut into 24 pieces.

red velvet brownies

YIELD 9 brownies

PREP 20 minutes

BAKE 30 minutes

RED VELVET BROWNIES

Signature Brownie recipe for
8 × 8-inch pan (page 19)

1 tablespoon red food coloring

1 teaspoon white vinegar

CREAM CHEESE FROSTING

½ cup (4 ounces) cream cheese, at
room temperature

2 tablespoons salted butter, softened

½ cup confectioners' sugar

½ teaspoon pure vanilla extract

Some say red velvet cake was first served at New York City's Waldorf Astoria hotel in the 1930s. Others believe it was created at the bakery of Eaton's department store in Winnepeg, Canada. Whatever its origin, the crimson-colored batter that gives red velvet cake its name is showing up in all sorts of desserts these days. Why not use it in brownies? This recipe combines the rich chocolate taste red velvet cake is famous for with the fudgy texture of my Signature Brownies. Topped with cream cheese frosting, it's a tasty twist on one of the world's legendary cakes!

1. Preheat the oven to 350°F. Grease an 8 × 8-inch pan and set aside.

2. **PREPARE THE RED VELVET BROWNIES:** Melt the chocolate chips and butter on high in a microwave-safe bowl for 30 seconds; remove and stir. Return to the microwave and heat in 15-second intervals until smooth and creamy.

3. Use an electric mixer set on lowest setting or spatula to mix together the eggs, vanilla, and sugar in a separate bowl. Blend the egg mixture into the melted chocolate until well combined.

4. Add the food coloring and vinegar to the chocolate mixture and mix well.

5. Mix in the flour, baking powder, salt, and cocoa powder until thoroughly blended.

6. Pour the batter into the prepared pan and bake for 30 minutes, until center rises and falls and edges begin to crisp. Set aside to cool.

7. **PREPARE THE CREAM CHEESE FROSTING:** Using an electric mixer, blend the cream cheese and butter together on medium speed. Add the confectioners' sugar and vanilla and continue mixing, scraping down the bowl with a spatula as needed, until the frosting is smooth and creamy.

8. Spread the cream cheese frosting over the brownies after they are completely cooled and cut into 9 squares.

macaroon brownies

YIELD	9 brownies
PREP	20 minutes
BAKE	35 to 40 minutes

Signature Brownie recipe for
8 × 8-inch pan (page 19)

COCONUT TOPPING

1 (14-ounce) bag flaked sweetened coconut

1 (14-ounce) can sweetened condensed milk

1 teaspoon pure vanilla extract

2 egg whites

¼ teaspoon salt

C hocolate and coconut go together like Bogart and Bacall, Antony and Cleopatra, Romeo and Juliet. In fact, there's something almost magical about the compatibility of these two flavors. With a brownie layer on the bottom and mini mounds of shredded coconut on top, this dessert is a joy to share—and tastes suspiciously like a beloved candy bar.

1. Preheat the oven to 350°F. Grease an 8 × 8-inch pan.

2. Prepare the signature brownie batter and pour into the prepared pan.

3. PREPARE THE COCONUT TOPPING: Combine all of the topping ingredients and mix thoroughly with a spatula.

4. Drop dollops of the topping with a tablespoon onto the brownie batter to cover the batter completely. Bake for 35 to 40 minutes, until the center is firm and the coconut peaks start to turn golden.

5. Cool completely, then cut into 9 pieces.

> The trick here is to make sure you whip the egg whites until they form stiff peaks.

salted caramel brownies

YIELD 9 brownies

PREP 20 minutes

BAKE 30 to 35 minutes

Signature Brownie recipe for
8 × 8-inch pan (page 19)

CARAMEL TOPPING

8 tablespoons (1 stick) salted butter

½ cup light brown sugar, packed

Flaked or coarse sea salt, for
sprinkling

W*ho doesn't love the combination of sweet and savory? Add chocolate to the equation (by now you know, there has to be chocolate), and you have my personal favorite!*

1. Preheat the oven to 350°F. Grease an 8 × 8-inch pan.

2. Prepare the signature brownie recipe, pour into the prepared pan and set aside.

3. PREPARE THE CARAMEL TOPPING: Melt the butter in a saucepan over medium heat. Add the brown sugar and stir constantly until the mixture is bubbly. Continue to stir for 2 to 3 minutes more, until the mixture begins to thicken and turns a light golden color.

4. Pour the caramel topping on top of the brownie batter as evenly as possible. The caramel mixture spreads during baking, so don't be concerned if there are exposed areas of brownie batter.

5. Bake for 30 to 35 minutes, until center is set. Remove the pan from the oven and immediately sprinkle the top of the brownies with sea salt. (See option below.)

6. Let cool completely, then cut into 9 squares.

OPTION: To make these brownies even more scrumptious, prepare a chocolate drizzle using ½ cup (3 ounces) of semisweet chocolate chips and ¼ teaspoon of vegetable shortening or coconut oil. In a microwave-safe bowl, microwave the chocolate chips and shortening on high for 30 seconds; remove and stir. If the chocolate chips are not completely melted, microwave in 15-second intervals until smooth and creamy. (Do not overheat or the chocolate will scorch.) Drizzle the melted chocolate over the cooled brownies before slicing.

peanut butter cup brownies

YIELD	9 brownies
PREP	15 minutes
BAKE	35 to 40 minutes

Signature Brownie recipe for 8 × 8-inch pan (page 19)

PEANUT BUTTER TOPPING

1 cup creamy peanut butter (all-natural recommended)

½ cup light brown sugar, packed

hese brownies are a spin on that famous chocolate and peanut butter cup. Now, my philosophy is if you're going to indulge, use only the best ingredients. That's why I always reach for all-natural peanut butter. It makes all the difference. All-natural peanut butter should have one ingredient: peanuts! There are several national brands that offer "real" peanut butter. Many supermarkets also grind their own natural peanut butter and stock it near the deli counter. Because the peanut oil rises to the top, be sure to mix your peanut butter thoroughly before adding it to the recipe.

1. Preheat the oven to 350°F. Grease an 8 × 8-inch pan.

2. Prepare the signature brownie batter and pour it into the prepared pan.

3. **MAKE THE PEANUT BUTTER TOPPING:** Mix all the ingredients together using a spatula; the consistency should be chunky.

4. Use a tablespoon to drop dollops of the peanut butter topping evenly on top of brownie batter.

5. Bake for 35 to 40 minutes, until center is set.

6. Cool completely, then cut into 9 squares.

kahlúa® and cream brownies

YIELD	24 brownies
PREP	20 minutes
BAKE	35 to 40 minutes

*F*udgy chocolate with a hint of Kahlúa® and a swirl of cream cheese, this recipe rolls three indulgences into one heavenly square. Be daring and partner these brownies with after-dinner cordials.

BROWNIE LAYER

3 cups (18 ounces) semisweet chocolate chips

9 tablespoons (1 stick plus 1 tablespoon) salted butter

3 large eggs

1½ teaspoons pure vanilla extract

¾ cup sugar

1 cup all-purpose flour

¾ teaspoon baking powder

¼ teaspoon salt, heaping

1½ tablespoons 100% baking cocoa

¼ cup Kahlúa® or other coffee-flavored liqueur

CREAM CHEESE SWIRL

1 (8-ounce) package cream cheese, at room temperature

4 tablespoons salted butter, softened

¼ cup sugar

1 large egg

1 tablespoon Kahlúa® or other coffee-flavored liqueur

1. Preheat the oven to 350°F. Grease a 9 × 13-inch pan and set aside.

2. **PREPARE THE BROWNIE LAYER:** Microwave chocolate chips and butter in a large microwave-safe bowl on high for 30 seconds; remove and stir. Return to the microwave if not completely melted and microwave in 15-second intervals until smooth and creamy. (Do not overheat or the chocolate will scorch.)

3. Use an electric mixer set on lowest speed or a spatula to mix the eggs, vanilla, and sugar in a separate bowl until well combined. Blend the egg mixture into the melted chocolate mixture. Add the flour, baking powder, salt, and cocoa and mix until thoroughly combined. Pour the brownie batter into the prepared pan and set aside.

4. **PREPARE THE CREAM CHEESE SWIRL:** Use an electric mixer set on lowest speed to blend the cream cheese with the softened butter. Add the sugar, egg, and Kahlúa® and mix thoroughly.

5. Use a tablespoon to drop evenly spaced dollops of the cream cheese mixture on top of the brownie batter. Swirl the cream cheese mixture with a butter knife into the brownie batter to create a marbled effect.

6. Bake for 35 to 40 minutes, until the center is firm and the edges begin to turn golden. Cool completely, and then cut into 24 pieces.

Kahlúa® is a registered trademark of The Absolut Company Aktiebolag

bacon and bourbon brownies

YIELD   9 brownies

PREP   25 minutes

BAKE   30 to 35 minutes

¼ cup bourbon

½ cup coarsely chopped pecans

Signature Brownie recipe for
8 × 8-inch pan (page 19)

½ cup chopped cooked bacon
(it should be crisp)

*S*uddenly everything is being paired with bacon. There's bacon-infused vodka, bacon ice cream; I've even seen bacon-flavored lip balm. I don't know who or what started the bacon boom, but I say kudos! And then, as always, I figure out how to get chocolate into the mix. The result is this tasty collaboration. The saltiness of the bacon and the nuttiness of the pecans complement the sweetness of the chocolate, and the hint of bourbon adds a certain grown-up appeal. Serve them at your next barbecue or TV-watch party.

1. Preheat the oven to 350°F. Grease an 8 × 8-inch pan and set aside.

2. Pour the bourbon over the chopped pecans and set aside to allow the nuts to absorb the bourbon while you make the brownie batter.

3. Prepare the signature brownie recipe, pour the batter into the prepared pan and set aside.

4. Drain the pecans in a colander to remove the excess bourbon. Spread them out on a baking sheet and toast them in the preheated oven for 10 minutes. Mix the toasted pecans with the chopped bacon and evenly sprinkle the mixture over the brownie batter.

5. Bake for 30 to 35 minutes, until edges are crisp. Cool completely, and then cut into 9 brownies.

> I take shortcuts whenever possible, as long as they don't affect quality. For this recipe, I buy bacon that's already cooked and ready for the microwave.

apple blondies with white chocolate chips

YIELD 24 blondies

PREP 10 to 15 minutes

BAKE 25 to 27 minutes

12 tablespoons (1½ sticks) salted butter, melted

1½ cups light brown sugar, packed

2 large eggs

2 teaspoons pure vanilla extract

1½ cups all-purpose flour

1 teaspoon baking powder

½ teaspoon salt

2 cups peeled and finely chopped apples

1 cup (6 ounces) white chocolate chips

1 cup chopped pecans or walnuts, optional

*A*pples are at their peak in the fall. That's why, around Halloween, you see trays of them candy-coated with chocolate or caramel in confectioners' windows. Just such a display was the inspiration for this recipe—I had a sneaking suspicion that adding apples and sweet, creamy white chocolate to my Blonde Brownie recipe would make for a surprisingly delicious combination. And, boy, was I right! Making a pan of these brownies is a lovely way to invite autumn inside.

Like a little crunch in your brownies? Add a cup of chopped pecans or walnuts when you fold the apples and white chocolate chips into the batter.

1. Preheat the oven to 325°F. Grease a 9 × 13-inch pan and set aside.

2. Use an electric mixer set on the lowest speed or a spatula to combine the melted butter and brown sugar and mix thoroughly. Mix in the eggs and vanilla until well combined. Add the flour, baking powder, and salt and mix thoroughly.

3. Fold in the chopped apple, white chocolate chips, and nuts, if using, with a spatula, distributing them evenly in the batter.

4. Spread the batter into the prepared pan and bake for 25 to 27 minutes, until the edges are slightly brown and the top is golden.

5. Cool completely, and then and cut into 24 pieces.

peanut butter and jelly brownies

YIELD	24 brownies
PREP	20 minutes
BAKE	35 to 40 minutes

12 tablespoons (1½ sticks) salted butter, softened

1½ cups light brown sugar, packed

¾ cup chunky-style peanut butter (all-natural recommended)

2 large eggs

2 teaspoons pure vanilla extract

1½ cups all-purpose flour

1 teaspoon baking powder

½ teaspoon salt

1 cup (6 ounces) semisweet chocolate chips

¾ cup strawberry jelly

*W*hat could be better than a PB&J sandwich in your kid's lunchbox (or yours for that matter)? How about a PB&JB? That's a peanut butter brownie with jelly! The flavor combination of peanut butter, chocolate, and strawberry really rocks. Elvis Presley might even have been tempted to give up his legendary peanut butter and banana combo for one of these.

1. Preheat the oven to 325°F. Grease a 9 × 13-inch pan and set aside.

2. Use an electric mixer on medium speed to beat the butter, brown sugar, and peanut butter until well mixed. Add the eggs and vanilla and mix well. Add the flour, baking powder, and salt and mix thoroughly. Fold in the chocolate chips using a spatula.

3. Spread the batter evenly in the prepared pan. Drop dollops of the strawberry jelly evenly over the batter using a tablespoon. Use a butter knife to swirl the jelly into the batter to create a marbled effect.

4. Bake for 35 to 40 minutes, until a toothpick inserted in the center comes out clean.

5. Cool completely, and then cut into 24 pieces.

brownie filling

YIELD   2 cups

PREP   5 minutes

1 (14-ounce) can sweetened condensed milk

12 tablespoons (1½ sticks) salted butter, melted

2 teaspoons pure vanilla extract

1 cup 100% baking cocoa

¾ cup all-purpose flour

ecause this filling is egg-free, it need not be baked, and may be used in many ways. See my recipes for Brownie-stuffed Crêpes (page 53), Brownie-filled French Toast (page 54), Brownie-filled Doughnut Holes (page 51), "Brownie-fied" Strawberries (page 172), "Haute" Chocolate (page 185), and Brownie Bread Pudding (page 62). Or use your imagination to create other sweet treats that take advantage of the fudge filling.

1. Blend the sweetened condensed milk with the melted butter. Mix in the vanilla. Add the cocoa and flour and mix thoroughly. Allow to cool; texture will be exactly like a brownie batter.

2. Store in an airtight container in the refrigerator for up to one month. Bring to room temperature before using.

brownies for breakfast

At our house, weekday mornings are a race, but weekends unwind at a slower pace. Here are a dozen recipes that transform everyday breakfasts into mini celebrations. They're all special enough for a fancy brunch, and four of them use brownie filling that can be made ahead for those days when you have to dash. Can you think of a sweeter way to start your day than with Chocolate Chip Biscuits or Brownie Pancakes?

brownie pancakes

YIELD	16 pancakes
PREP	15 minutes
COOK	2 to 4 minutes per batch

Signature Brownie recipe for
8 × 8-inch pan (page 19)

1½ cups biscuit mix

1 cup milk

When my daughter, Rachael, used to have sleepovers, I liked to cook breakfast for her and her gang of girlfriends. I would run down the menu choices for them: eggs…cereal…bagels…oatmeal, but it wasn't until I called out "brownie pancakes" that all those tiny hands shot up in the air.

And just to make it more fun, I always offered a selection of toppings so every girl could customize her own pancakes. Chocolate, butterscotch, or peanut butter chips; whipped cream, chocolate sauce, peanut butter sauce, or even maple syrup. When it comes to the toppings, use your imagination. Then watch as these fly off the platter like, well, hotcakes.

1. Preheat an electric griddle to 300°F or place a nonstick pan over medium-high heat.

2. Prepare the signature brownie batter according to the recipe. Stir in the biscuit mix and milk until well blended.

3. Scoop ¼ cup of batter per pancake on the griddle or pan and cook them until the edges are dry and the centers are bubbly, about 2 minutes. Flip the pancakes and continue cooking for another 1 to 2 minutes, until you see a solid baked surface.

4. Transfer the pancakes to a plate and repeat with the remaining batter. Serve hot with your favorite toppings.

True chocolate lovers like me can't resist adding chocolate chips to pancakes. To ensure even coverage, don't add them to the batter. Instead, sprinkle them on one side of the pancakes once they're in the pan, let them sink in, then flip the pancakes.

brownie waffles

YIELD   6 waffles

PREP   9 to 10 minutes

BAKE   3 minutes per waffle

SPECIAL EQUIPMENT

Waffle iron

2 cups (12 ounces) semisweet chocolate chips

6 tablespoons salted butter

4 large eggs

1 teaspoon pure vanilla extract

½ cup sugar

¾ cup all-purpose flour

½ teaspoon baking powder

¼ teaspoon salt

1 tablespoon 100% baking cocoa

Confectioners' sugar, for sprinkling

Somehow waffles turn any breakfast into a special occasion. That's why at our house, we save them for Sunday mornings. Time seems to slow down as everyone waits for the waffle iron to work its magic. To me, a waffle for breakfast is the ideal antidote to our hurry-up world—especially when it tastes like a brownie.

There are as many toppings for waffles as there are cultures that serve them. These include fresh fruit, whipped cream, maple syrup, cheese, eggs, caramel sauce—even bacon. Since this recipe includes butter and, of course, chocolate, I like to keep the topping simple—a light dusting of confectioners' sugar is all you need.

1. Preheat the waffle iron to medium heat.

2. Microwave the chocolate chips and butter in a large microwave-safe bowl on high for 30 seconds; remove and stir. Return to microwave if not completely melted, and microwave in 15-second intervals until smooth and creamy. (Do not overheat or the chocolate will scorch.)

3. Mix together the eggs, vanilla, and sugar in a separate bowl until well combined. Add the egg mixture to the chocolate mixture and stir until smooth. Add the flour, baking powder, salt, and cocoa and mix until the batter is smooth.

4. Drop about 2 tablespoons of batter into each section of the preheated waffle iron and cook for 2 to 3 minutes. Let cool before lifting the waffles from the iron; set aside. Repeat with the remaining batter.

5. Sprinkle the waffles with confectioners' sugar and serve warm.

brownie doughnuts

YIELD 12 doughnuts

PREP 15 minutes

BAKE 12 minutes per batch

SPECIAL EQUIPMENT
  6-count doughnut pan

*W*ouldn't you rather stay in your PJs on Saturday morning instead of racing to the doughnut shop? Now you can! In less time than it takes to get dressed and walk the dog, you can have homemade doughnuts cooling on the counter. And these aren't just any doughnuts—they're rich, chocolatey brownie doughnuts! Plus, you can sweeten the deal with your favorite toppings.

2 cups (12 ounces) semisweet chocolate chips

6 tablespoons salted butter

3 large eggs

1 teaspoon pure vanilla extract

½ cup sugar

½ cup all-purpose flour

½ teaspoon baking powder

¼ teaspoon salt

1 tablespoon 100% baking cocoa

Melted chocolate, candy sprinkles, or confectioners' sugar, for garnish

1. Preheat the oven to 350°F. Grease the doughnut pan with nonstick cooking spray and set aside.

2. Microwave the chocolate chips and butter in a large microwave-safe bowl for 30 seconds; remove and stir. Return to microwave if not completely melted, and microwave in 15-second intervals until smooth and creamy. (Do not overheat or the chocolate will scorch.)

3. Mix together the eggs, vanilla, and sugar in a separate bowl until well combined. Add the egg mixture to the chocolate mixture and stir until smooth. Add the flour, baking powder, salt, and cocoa and mix thoroughly.

4. Pour about ¼ cup of batter into each cavity of the prepared doughnut pan. Bake for 12 minutes, until a toothpick inserted halfway into the donut comes out clean. Allow to cool until pan is warm enough to handle, about 3 to 5 minutes, before removing the doughnuts. Repeat with the remaining batter.

5. Garnish the doughnuts with melted chocolate, sprinkles, confectioners' sugar, or your favorite combination.

brownie-filled doughnut holes

YIELD   24 doughnut holes

PREP   40 minutes

BAKE   10 to 15 minutes

SPECIAL EQUIPMENT

24-count doughnut hole pan or
mini muffin pan; pastry bag with
narrow nozzle

*hese are super for when neighbors come by to watch football. No plates or forks
required. If quizzed about what they are, just say offhandedly, "Oh, plain old
doughnut holes." Then watch their faces light up as they take their first bite and the
fudgy brownie flavor fills their mouths. Guaranteed high fives all around.*

DOUGHNUT HOLE BATTER

1 cup self-rising flour (or all-purpose
flour plus ½ teaspoon baking soda)

1 tablespoon sugar

1 teaspoon baking powder

¼ teaspoon salt

2 tablespoons canola oil

1 large egg

2 teaspoons pure vanilla extract

½ cup low-fat (1%) milk or almond milk

1 cup Brownie Filling (recipe, page 43),
at room temperature

CINNAMON-SUGAR COATING

⅓ cup sugar

2 teaspoons ground cinnamon

1 tablespoon salted butter, melted

1. Preheat the oven to 350°F. Grease the doughnut hole pan or mini muffin pan with nonstick cooking spray. Wipe off excess oil with a paper towel and set aside.

2. **PREPARE THE DOUGHNUT HOLE BATTER:** Whisk together the flour, sugar, baking powder, and salt. Make a well in the center of the dry ingredients and add the oil, egg, vanilla, and milk. Whisk the batter until smooth and lump-free.

3. Spoon about 2 teaspoons of the batter into each section of the pan, filling them three-quarters full.

4. Bake the doughnut holes, checking after 10 minutes and every minute thereafter, until they are golden in color and a toothpick inserted into the center comes out clean. Allow the doughnut holes to cool for 5 minutes in the pan, then transfer them to a cooling rack.

5. **PREPARE THE CINNAMON-SUGAR COATING:** Mix together the sugar and cinnamon for the coating in a shallow bowl.

6. Brush each cooled doughnut with a light coating of the melted butter. Roll each doughnut hole in the cinnamon-sugar until evenly coated.

7. Fill a pastry bag with the brownie filling. Use a narrow nozzle to pipe the brownie filling into the center of each doughnut hole, filling it until the doughnut puffs up and expands. (Don't overfill or the doughnut holes will overflow.)

"brownie-fied" cinnamon rolls

YIELD	15 servings
PREP	40 minutes
RISE	Two 1-hour periods
BAKE	25 to 30 minutes

DOUGH

¼ cup plus 1 teaspoon granulated sugar

1 (¼-ounce) package active dry yeast

½ cup warm water (110°F)

½ cup milk

4 tablespoons (½ stick) salted butter

1 teaspoon salt

2 large eggs, beaten

4 cups all-purpose flour

BROWN SUGAR AND ORANGE ZEST GLAZE

6 tablespoons salted butter

¾ cup light brown sugar, packed

1 tablespoon orange zest

CINNAMON AND CHOCOLATE FILLING

4 tablespoons (½ stick) salted butter

¾ cup light brown sugar, packed

1 tablespoon ground cinnamon

1 tablespoon 100% baking cocoa

GARNISH

1 cup BROWNIE BRITTLE™ (one 5-ounce bag = 1 cup crushed) or chocolate wafers crushed in a food processor

4 tablespoons (½ stick) salted butter, melted

Unless you're an early riser (pardon the pun), you might want to save this recipe for a brunch day. That's because you have to allow the dough to rise twice, which takes an hour or two. However, I assure you these fluffy, yeasty cinnamon buns, with a hint of orange, are well worth the wait. Meanwhile, you can prepare the rest of your brunch menu and set the table. If you plan it right, your guests will arrive just as the oven timer dings. Tell me, who doesn't like being greeted by the aroma of cinnamon and chocolate?

1. **PREPARE DOUGH:** In a small bowl, dissolve 1 teaspoon of the sugar and the yeast in the warm water. Set aside.

2. Warm the milk in a small saucepan until it bubbles, then remove from the heat. Mix the remaining ¼ cup sugar, the butter, and salt into the warm milk; stir until the butter melts. Let cool until lukewarm.

3. Combine the yeast mixture, milk mixture, eggs, and 1½ cups of the flour. Stir well to combine. Add in the remaining 2½ cups flour, ½ cup at a time, beating well after each addition.

4. Turn the dough onto a lightly floured surface. Once it comes together, knead until smooth and elastic, about 8 minutes. Place the dough in a large, lightly oiled bowl and turn to coat with the oil. Cover with a damp cloth and let rise in a warm place until doubled in volume, about 1 hour. Grease a 9 × 13-inch baking pan and set aside.

5. **PREPARE BROWN SUGAR AND ORANGE ZEST GLAZE:** Melt the butter in a small saucepan over medium heat. Stir in the brown sugar, whisking until smooth; stir in the orange zest. Pour the mixture into the prepared pan.

6. **PREPARE CINNAMON AND CHOCOLATE FILLING:** Melt butter; set aside. Mix brown sugar, cinnamon, and cocoa in a bowl; set aside.

7. Turn the dough onto a lightly floured surface. Use a rolling pin to roll the dough into an 18 × 14-inch rectangle. Brush the dough with 2 tablespoons of the melted butter, leaving a ½-inch border unbuttered; sprinkle the buttered dough with the brown sugar, cinnamon, and cocoa mixture. Start at long side and tightly roll up the dough into a log, pinching the seam to seal. Brush with the remaining 2 tablespoons melted butter. Slice the log into 15 pieces using a serrated knife. Place the pieces, cut-side down, in the prepared pan. Cover and let rise for 1 hour, or until doubled in volume.

8. Preheat the oven to 375°F. Bake for 25 to 30 minutes, until the rolls are golden brown. Let cool in the pan for 3 minutes, then invert onto a serving platter. Scrape any remaining brown sugar and orange zest glaze from the bottom of the pan onto the rolls.

9. **PREPARE THE GARNISH:** Mix the crushed BROWNIE BRITTLE™ with the melted butter and sprinkle over the cinnamon rolls. Serve warm!

brownie-stuffed crêpes

YIELD	18 to 20 crêpes
PREP	20 minutes
COOK	30 to 40 seconds per crêpe

Crêpe is a French word that comes from the Latin term "crispa," which means curled. These light, delicate pancakes are so named because their edges curl when they hit the heat. So what makes my version of these thin wrappers special? The creamy brownie filling. Serve the crêpes warm with a dusting of confectioners' sugar to make a lasting impression.

CRÊPE BATTER

2 large eggs

¾ cup milk

½ cup water

1 teaspoon pure vanilla extract

1 cup all-purpose flour

3 tablespoons salted butter, melted, plus more butter for the pan

BROWNIE FILLING

1 cup Brownie Filling (page 43), at room temperature

1 to 2 teaspoons milk

Confectioners' sugar, for dusting

1. Combine all the ingredients for the crêpe batter in a blender and mix on high speed for 15 seconds until the batter is smooth. Refrigerate for about 1 hour, until well chilled.

2. Prepare the brownie filling according to instructions (or use leftover brownie filling, if available). Add the milk to 1 cup of the brownie filling and mix until creamy.

3. Preheat the oven to 250°F. Heat a small nonstick pan over medium heat and melt 1 tablespoon butter to coat the bottom.

4. Pour 2 tablespoons of the chilled crêpe batter into the pan and quickly swirl it to coat the bottom of the pan. Cook the crêpe for approximately 30 seconds and flip it. Cook for another 10 seconds on the second side, then slide the crêpe onto a plate. Keep cooked crêpes warm in the preheated oven.

5. Scoop 1 tablespoon of the brownie filling into the center of the crêpe, and then fold both sides inward. Slide the crêpe onto a plate.

6. Cook and fill the remaining crêpes as described in steps 3 through 5 until you've used up all the batter. Serve warm, dusted with the confectioners' sugar.

brownie-filled french toast

YIELD   4 servings

PREP   20 minutes

COOK   3 to 4 minutes per batch

Brownie Filling recipe (page 43)

6 large eggs

¼ cup milk

8 slices dense bread, such as white or challah

3 tablespoons salted butter

Whipped cream and strawberries or maple syrup, for serving

One day, while preparing brunch for out-of-town guests, I remembered that I had leftover brownie filling in the fridge. Since I firmly believe everything's better with chocolate, I spread the filling on some bread and made a French toast sandwich. I knew I had a winner when my guests said it deserved to be on the menu at a fancy resort.

1. Prepare the brownie filling according to instructions; set aside.

2. Lightly whisk the eggs and milk in a shallow bowl until combined.

3. Spread the brownie filling in between the slices of bread to create 4 sandwiches. (See note below.) Dip each sandwich into the egg-milk mixture briefly to coat.

4. Melt the butter in a heavy skillet over medium-high heat. When the skillet is hot, brown the sandwiches until golden on both sides, 3 to 4 minutes total.

5. Serve topped with whipped cream and strawberries, or drizzle with maple syrup.

NOTE: There may be enough leftover brownie filling to make 1 or 2 more sandwiches, or you can store it in an airtight container in the refrigerator for up to one month. Bring to room temperature before using.

brownie banana bread

YIELD	9 to 12 bars
PREP	15 minutes
BAKE	30 minutes

2 cups (12 ounces) semisweet chocolate chips

6 tablespoons salted butter

3 large eggs

1 teaspoon pure vanilla extract

½ cup sugar

¾ cup all-purpose flour

½ teaspoon baking powder

¼ teaspoon salt

1 tablespoon 100% baking cocoa

1 cup (6 ounces) milk or semisweet chocolate chips

2 ripe bananas, mashed

¼ cup confectioners' sugar, for dusting

The idea for this recipe popped into my head as I was remembering the frozen chocolate-covered bananas my mom let my sister Judi and I make when we were kids. We'd dip the bananas in melted chocolate and then roll them in chopped nuts or coconut (or whatever was left over from Mom's most recent baking effort). We loved them!

My reminiscence inspired me to create something different using the blissfully compatible banana-chocolate combination. It was going to be warm. It would cozy up to a hot cup of coffee. And unlike traditional banana bread that's baked in a loaf pan and sliced, it would be bar-shaped. The result: An extreme makeover of the frozen banana treat of my childhood that's every bit as memorable.

1. Preheat the oven to 350°F. Grease an 8 × 8-inch pan and set aside.

2. Microwave 2 cups of the semisweet chocolate chips and the butter in a microwave-safe bowl on high for 30 seconds; remove and stir. Return to the microwave if not completely melted, and microwave in 15-second intervals until smooth and creamy. Do not overheat.

3. Mix the eggs, vanilla, and sugar in a separate bowl. Blend the egg mixture into melted chocolate mixture. Add the flour, baking powder, salt, and cocoa; mix until well combined. Add the mashed bananas and mix thoroughly. Add the 1 cup semisweet or milk chocolate chips and stir to evenly distribute. Pour the batter into the prepared pan and bake for 30 minutes, or until the top is set. Allow to cool.

4. Cut into desired number of servings, dust with confectioners' sugar, and serve.

chocolate chip biscuits

YIELD   18 small biscuits

PREP   15 minutes

BAKE   12 to 15 minutes

2 cups all-purpose flour

1 tablespoon baking powder

1 tablespoon sugar

½ teaspoon salt

8 tablespoons (1 stick) salted butter, chilled and cut into small pieces

¾ cup milk

½ cup (3 ounces) mini semisweet chocolate chips

I nstead of coffeecake or cheese pastries for breakfast, how about some piping hot biscuits to go with your bacon and eggs next weekend? These moist drop biscuits, with chocolate chips inside, are a welcome change from the plain ready-made ones you find in the dairy case. No need to put the butter dish on the table either. Just split one open, watch the steam escape, and take a bite of butter and chocolate bliss. What a delicious way to start your day.

1. Preheat the oven to 400°F. Grease a baking sheet with butter or nonstick cooking spray and set aside.

2. Mix the flour, baking powder, sugar, and salt. Add the butter to the flour mixture. Chop and mix with a pastry blade until the mixture becomes a coarse batter. Mix in the milk gradually until the batter becomes sticky. Stir in the chocolate chips by hand.

3. Drop the batter onto the prepared baking sheet using a teaspoon. Bake for 12 to 15 minutes, until the peaks and edges begin to turn golden. Serve warm.

brownie scones

YIELD	12 to 16 scones
PREP	15 minutes
BAKE	16 to 18 minutes

SPECIAL EQUIPMENT

9-inch round- or heart-shaped cookie cutter

2 cups all-purpose flour

¾ cup 100% baking cocoa

½ cup sugar

1 tablespoon baking powder

1 teaspoon salt

12 tablespoons (1½ sticks) salted butter, chilled

1 cup buttermilk

1 teaspoon pure vanilla extract

½ cup (3 ounces) semisweet chocolate chips

1 large egg

2 teaspoons water

Coarse sea salt

Scones are said to have originated in Scotland in the early 1500s. Legend has it that Scottish kings were once crowned at the Stone of Destiny (or Scone), and that's how this single-serving quick bread got its name. It seems odd that such a flaky, moist taste treat would be named after a rock! A little denser than a biscuit, these bonny brownie scones are delicious with coffee or tea and a welcome addition to a holiday brunch.

1. Preheat the oven to 400°F. Grease a baking sheet with butter and set aside.

2. Whisk together the flour, cocoa, sugar, baking powder, and salt in a large mixing bowl. Cut the butter into small chunks using a pastry cutter or knife, and work them into the flour mixture to create a coarse batter.

3. Mix the buttermilk with the vanilla and fold it into the batter until the batter is pliable but not dry. Add the chocolate chips and mix until evenly distributed.

4. Sprinkle flour onto a work surface and, using a rolling pin, roll out the batter until ½ inch thick. Cut out 12 to 16 scones using a round- or heart-shaped cookie cutter. Arrange them on the prepared baking sheet.

5. Mix together the egg and water and brush the surface of the scones with the egg wash. Sprinkle the scones with sea salt. Bake for 16 to 18 minutes, until a toothpick inserted into the scones comes out clean. Allow to cool until pan is warm to the touch.

brownie bread pudding

YIELD   6 servings

PREP   30 to 35 minutes

BAKE   45 to 50 minutes

Unsalted butter for greasing pan

Brownie Filling recipe (page 43)

12 slices brioche bread or challah, at least 1 day old

PUDDING MIXTURE

2 cups light cream

¼ teaspoon salt

1 teaspoon pure vanilla extract

1 cup sugar

3 large eggs

Several years ago, I was invited to a friend's house for brunch. When I asked what I could bring, she replied without even taking a breath, "Why dessert, of course. That's your specialty!" Wow! No pressure, right? Now, I had to come up with something different, something spectacular.

Hmmm, I thought. Bread pudding is pretty popular. I bet if I "brownied" it up a bit, it would pass muster. Well, my bread pudding never even made it to the dessert table. It was served along with the main course, and there wasn't a crumb left when it was time for coffee and sweets. I took my empty bowl home—with my brownie queen reputation still intact.

1. Preheat the oven to 350°F. Grease an 8 × 8-inch baking dish with unsalted butter.

2. Prepare the brownie filling according to directions. Spread it on 6 slices of the bread, then top each one with another slice of bread to form 6 sandwiches. Cut each sandwich into 6 to 8 pieces and pile the sandwich pieces into the greased baking dish.

3. **PREPARE THE PUDDING MIXTURE:** Combine the cream, salt, and vanilla in a small saucepan; cook over medium heat until warm. Whisk together the sugar and eggs. Add the cream mixture to the egg mixture gradually, stirring constantly to make sure the eggs do not cook.

4. Pour the pudding mixture over the bread pieces and cover the dish with aluminum foil. Bake on the center rack of the oven for 45 to 50 minutes. Remove the foil after about 20 minutes and check every few minutes until golden brown on top. Allow the pudding to rest at least 10 minutes before serving.

brownie bars

What I love about brownie bars is their versatility. Line the pan with a butter-and-chocolate crust to add a little crunch. Top them with a chocolate drizzle, confectioners' sugar, whipped cream, coconut—the options seem endless. Take them camping, picnicking, to a friend's house. They're easy to pack up and they travel well. Plus, you can cut them into mini or mighty portions, depending on the size of the crowd. Sure can't do all that with cake or pie!

double-nut brownie brittle™ squares with moonshine whipped cream

YIELD	48 to 50 squares
PREP	25 minutes
BAKE	25 to 30 minutes
SPECIAL EQUIPMENT	
	9 × 13-inch glass baking dish

BROWNIE BRITTLE™ CRUST

2 cups BROWNIE BRITTLE™
(one 5-ounce bag = 1 cup crushed)
or chocolate wafers crushed in
a food processor

8 tablespoons (1 stick) unsalted
butter, melted

DOUBLE-NUT FILLING

8 tablespoons (1 stick) unsalted
butter, melted

½ cup light brown sugar, packed

6 tablespoons honey

2 tablespoons granulated sugar

2 tablespoons heavy cream

¼ teaspoon salt

1 cup (4 ounces) pecan halves

1 cup (4 ounces) walnuts, chopped

½ teaspoon pure vanilla extract

1 tablespoon freshly minced orange zest

MOONSHINE WHIPPED CREAM

1 cup heavy cream

2 teaspoons confectioners' sugar

1 tablespoon Original Moonshine® Corn
Whiskey or bourbon, optional

*W*hoopi Goldberg hosts the "Chicken Coupe" at New York's Wine and Food Festival to benefit hunger relief organizations in New York City. This walk-around tasting features superstar chefs, celebrities, dozens of fried chicken variations, comfort-food sides, and chilled champagne. Imagine my excitement when I was invited to create an original dessert for the festival. My mind was buzzing: It had to have chocolate, and nuts would be nice. It should be easy to eat, because people would be standing, and it needed an element of surprise—moonshine whipped cream ought to do it! Anyway, this recipe was what I came up with. (Of course, I had to double it about 500 times to serve the festival's more than 55,000 guests!)

1. Arrange a rack in the center of the oven. Preheat the oven to 350°F.

2. **PREPARE THE BROWNIE BRITTLE™ CRUST:** Combine the BROWNIE BRITTLE™ and the melted butter, and mix thoroughly. Press the crumb mixture firmly and evenly into a 9 × 13-inch glass baking dish. Bake for 8 minutes. Transfer the pan to a wire rack to cool completely. Reduce the oven temperature to 325°F.

3. **PREPARE THE DOUBLE-NUT FILLING:** In a medium saucepan, combine the butter, brown sugar, honey, granulated sugar, cream, and salt. Bring to a boil over high heat, stirring constantly until the mixture coats the back of a spoon, about 1 minute. Remove the pan from the heat; stir in the nuts, vanilla, and orange zest. Pour the filling onto the cooled crust. Bake until the filling bubbles, 15 to 20 minutes. Transfer the pan to a wire rack to cool completely.

4. **PREPARE THE MOONSHINE WHIPPED CREAM, IF DESIRED:** Beat or whisk the cream, sugar, and whiskey, if using, until soft peaks form.

5. To serve, run a paring knife around the edges of the baking dish and cut the brownies into squares. Dip the brownies into the moonshine whipped cream and top with a dollop of remaining whipped cream. The bars can be stored in an airtight container for up to 1 week.
Original Moonshine® is a registered trademark of Stillhouse Spirits Co.

white chocolate-cherry macadamia nut squares

YIELD	24 bars
PREP	20 minutes
BAKE	33 to 38 minutes

BROWNIE BRITTLE™ CRUST

8 tablespoons (1 stick) salted butter, melted

2 cups BROWNIE BRITTLE™ (one 5-ounce bag = 1 cup crushed) or chocolate wafers crushed in a food processor

WHITE CHOCOLATE–CHERRY MACADAMIA FILLING

1 cup (6 ounces) white chocolate chips

1 cup (4 ounces) macadamia nuts, chopped

1 cup sweetened flaked coconut

½ cup maraschino cherries, drained and chopped

1 (14-ounce) can sweetened condensed milk

WHITE CHOCOLATE DRIZZLE

½ cup (3 ounces) white chocolate chips

¼ teaspoon vegetable shortening or coconut oil

These crunchy, chewy squares of bliss elevate dessert bars to a whole new level. I mean, what's not to like? Kids love the cherry-coconut combination, and adults appreciate the subtle pairing of white chocolate and macadamia nuts. Serve them straight from the pan or stack them on a cake plate in a pretty pyramid. However you dish them up, it's a win-win for everybody—especially you.

1. Preheat the oven to 350°F. Grease a 9 × 13-inch pan.

2. **PREPARE THE BROWNIE BRITTLE™ CRUST:** Mix the crushed BROWNIE BRITTLE™ with the melted butter until well combined. Press the crumb mixture firmly and evenly into the bottom of the pan and bake for 8 minutes.

3. **PREPARE THE WHITE CHOCOLATE–CHERRY MACADAMIA FILLING:** Sprinkle the crust with the white chocolate chips, macadamia nuts, coconut, and cherries. Drizzle the sweetened condensed milk over all.

4. Bake for 25 to 30 minutes, until top turns golden. Cool completely.

5. **PREPARE THE WHITE CHOCOLATE DRIZZLE:** Microwave the white chocolate chips and shortening in a microwave-safe bowl on high for 30 seconds; remove and stir. Return to the microwave if not completely melted, and microwave in 15-second intervals, stirring until smooth and creamy. (Do not overheat or the chocolate will scorch.) Drizzle the white chocolate over the cooled bars before cutting them into 24 pieces.

chocolate-drizzled granola bars

YIELD	12 bars
PREP	15 minutes
BAKE	10 minutes (for toasting the oats)

3 cups old-fashioned oats

2 tablespoons canola oil

2 tablespoons light brown sugar

2 tablespoons agave or maple syrup

⅓ cup honey

1½ teaspoons pure vanilla extract

1 teaspoon ground cinnamon

¼ teaspoon ground nutmeg

½ cup BROWNIE BRITTLE™
(one 5-ounce bag = 1 cup crushed)
or chocolate wafers crushed in
a food processor

½ cup raisins

½ cup sunflower seeds

½ cup (3 ounces) semisweet
chocolate chips

SEMISWEET CHOCOLATE DRIZZLE

½ cup (3 ounces) semisweet
chocolate chips

¼ teaspoon vegetable shortening
or coconut oil

*W*hether you're heading out for a hike or brown bagging it to the office, these granola bars are made to travel—and provide an energizing lift during that midday slump. The oats, raisins, and sunflower seeds are fiber-rich; the honey, maple syrup, and spices wake up your taste buds; and the chocolate, well, that's just good for the soul.

1. Preheat the oven to 350°F. Line a 9 × 9-inch baking pan with parchment paper or foil, allowing two ends to overlap the side of the pan (this makes the bars easier to remove). Set aside.

2. Pour the oats into a 9 × 13-inch baking pan (or a baking sheet with a rim) and toast in the oven for 10 minutes, stirring occasionally to avoid burning.

3. Heat the canola oil in a small saucepan and add the brown sugar, agave, honey, vanilla, cinnamon, and nutmeg. Bring to a simmer over medium heat, stirring until well blended.

4. Transfer the toasted oats to a bowl. Pour in the warm, spicy syrup and mix thoroughly with a spatula. Add the crushed BROWNIE BRITTLE™, the raisins, sunflower seeds, and chocolate chips. Pour into the prepared pan and press to create an even layer. Refrigerate overnight or freeze for 1 hour.

5. Lift the two ends of the parchment to remove the bars from the pan when the granola bars are chilled. Cut into 12 rectangular bars by slicing the contents of the pan in half, then cutting each half into 6 portions.

6. PREPARE THE SEMISWEET CHOCOLATE DRIZZLE: Microwave the chocolate chips and shortening in a microwave-safe bowl for 30 seconds; remove and stir. Return to the microwave if not thoroughly melted, and microwave in 15-second intervals until smooth and creamy. (Do not overheat or the chocolate will scorch.)

7. Drizzle the melted chocolate on top of the bars and serve, or let the chocolate set, and then store the bars in an airtight container for up to a month.

key lime bars

YIELD	12 bars
PREP	15 minutes
BAKE	26 to 28 minutes

BROWNIE BRITTLE™ CRUST

1½ cups BROWNIE BRITTLE™
(one 5-ounce bag = 1 cup crushed)
or chocolate wafers crushed in
a food processor

6 tablespoons salted butter, melted

KEY LIME FILLING

¼ cup (2 ounces) cream cheese,
softened

1 tablespoon grated Key lime zest

1 (14-ounce) can sweetened
condensed milk

1 egg yolk

⅓ cup Key lime juice

Confectioners' sugar, for
sprinkling, optional

I f your prime rib dinner receives a standing ovation, your dessert certainly can't be a flop. These light, zesty bars are a refreshing complement to a hearty meal, and with only five ingredients, they come together in no time. Expect to hear requests for a repeat performance.

1. Preheat the oven to 325°F. Grease an 8 × 8-inch pan and set aside.

2. **PREPARE THE BROWNIE BRITTLE™ CRUST:** Mix the crushed BROWNIE BRITTLE™ and melted butter until well combined. Press firmly and evenly into the bottom of the prepared pan.

3. Bake for 10 minutes, until center is set. Set aside to cool.

4. **PREPARE THE KEY LIME FILLING:** Using an electric mixer or a spatula, mix together the cream cheese and lime zest until well combined. Stir in the sweetened condensed milk until blended. Add the egg yolk and lime juice and mix well.

5. Pour the filling over the partially cooled crust and bake for 16 to 18 minutes or until the top is set.

6. Sprinkle the bars with confectioners' sugar, if desired, and cut into 12 bars.

> If available, use real Key limes (they're yellow, smoother, and smaller than green Persian limes) or Key lime juice from Key West.

samoa brownie bars

YIELD 24 bars

PREP 20 minutes

BAKE 30 minutes

Signature Brownie recipe for
9 × 13-inch pan (page 19)

2½ cups sweetened flaked coconut

1 (12-ounce) can of dulce de leche

⅓ cup evaporated milk

SEMISWEET CHOCOLATE DRIZZLE
1 cup (6 ounces) semisweet
chocolate chips

¼ teaspoon vegetable shortening
or coconut oil

W henever I see "Samoa" in a recipe title, I immediately think "coconut." That's because coconut, along with other tropical fruits, is a staple of daily life on this Pacific island. Coconut milk, coconut meat, and flaked coconut appear in Samoan entrées and soups as well as desserts.

Because dulce de leche, which means "sweet milk" in Spanish, is such a delicious companion to coconut, I blend the two in this recipe. Then I spread this sweet, coconut-y concoction over the pan of brownies (which, as the story goes, are an American "invention"). And since there can never be too much of a good thing, I top it off with a semisweet chocolate drizzle. You could say these bars are like the United Nations of desserts.

1. Preheat the oven to 350°F. Grease or spray a 9 × 13-inch pan and set aside.

2. Prepare the signature brownie recipe according to directions, and bake for 30 minutes. Cool completely.

3. Spread the coconut flakes in a single layer on a baking sheet. Toast in the oven for 5 to 10 minutes, until flakes turn light brown.

4. In a microwave-safe bowl, blend the dulce de leche and evaporated milk; microwave in 30-second intervals until smooth and creamy. Stir in the coconut until evenly distributed. Spread the coconut filling over the cooled brownies.

5. **PREPARE THE SEMISWEET CHOCOLATE DRIZZLE:** Microwave the chocolate chips and shortening in a microwave-safe bowl on high for 30 seconds; remove and stir. Return to the microwave if not completely melted, and microwave in 15-second intervals until smooth and creamy. (Do not overheat or the chocolate will scorch).

6. Drizzle the bars with the melted chocolate and cut into 24 pieces.

white chocolate-raspberry cheesecake bars

YIELD	24 bars
PREP	15 minutes
BAKE	45 to 55 minutes

BROWNIE BRITTLE™ CRUST

2 cups BROWNIE BRITTLE™
(one 5-ounce bag = 1 cup crushed)
or chocolate wafers crushed in
a food processor

4 tablespoons (½ stick) salted
butter, melted

CHEESECAKE BATTER

3 (8-ounce) packages cream
cheese, softened

1 cup sugar

2 tablespoons all-purpose flour

3 large eggs

½ cup heavy cream

2 tablespoons pure vanilla extract

1 cup (6 ounces) white
chocolate chips

1 cup raspberry preserves

*I*f you think cheesecake is difficult to make or too highfalutin for your gang, try this recipe. The crunchy crust takes minutes to make, and the cheesecake batter blends fast and easy in a food processor. Plus, bars are so much simpler to cut and serve than traditional wedges of cheesecake. But don't let the simplicity fool you—the white chocolate adds an air of elegance, and the swirl of raspberry throughout makes these bars pretty as a picture. Not to mention super-licious!

1. Preheat the oven to 350°F. Grease a 9 × 13-inch pan and set aside.

2. **PREPARE THE BROWNIE BRITTLE™ CRUST:** Mix the crushed BROWNIE BRITTLE™ and melted butter until well combined. Press the crumb mixture firmly and evenly into the bottom of the prepared pan. Bake for 6 to 8 minutes. Allow to cool.

3. **PREPARE THE CHEESECAKE BATTER:** Beat cream cheese using a food processor. Add the sugar, flour, and eggs, and process on medium speed until well blended.

4. Using an electric mixer, beat the cream until stiff peaks form, stir in the vanilla, and fold into the cream cheese mixture. Gently mix in the white chocolate chips by hand until evenly dispersed.

5. Pour the cheesecake batter over the cooled crust. Drop the preserves by the spoonful over the cheesecake batter and swirl with a butter knife to create a marbled effect.

6. Bake for 40 to 45 minutes, until the center is set. Allow to cool before slicing and serving.

pistachio, coconut, and dried cranberry brownie brittle™ bars

YIELD	24 bars
PREP	20 minutes
BAKE	35 to 40 minutes

BROWNIE BRITTLE™ CRUST

2 cups BROWNIE BRITTLE™
(one 5-ounce bag = 1 cup crushed)
or chocolate wafers crushed in
a food processor

8 tablespoons (1 stick) salted
butter, melted

FILLING LAYER

1 cup (6 ounces) semisweet
chocolate chips

1 cup (4 ounces) pistachios, shelled

1 cup flaked sweetened coconut

1 cup dried cranberries

1 (14-ounce) can sweetened
condensed milk

SEMISWEET CHOCOLATE DRIZZLE

½ cup (3 ounces) semisweet
chocolate chips

¼ teaspoon vegetable shortening
or coconut oil

Your taste buds won't know what hit them. There's the buttery taste of pistachios, the sweetness of coconut, the tartness of cranberries, and the boldness of chocolate, all wrapped up in a neat little package. These bars are also a feast for the eyes. With pistachio green, cranberry red, white flecks of coconut, and dark chocolate, they're festive enough to grace any holiday table. By the way, did you know a pistachio is a member of the cashew family, and that dried cranberries are a tasty substitute for raisins in recipes?

1. Preheat the oven to 350°F. Grease a 9 × 13-inch pan.

2. **PREPARE THE CRUST:** Mix the crushed BROWNIE BRITTLE™ with the melted butter until well combined. Press the crumb mixture firmly and evenly into the bottom of the prepared pan. Bake for 8 minutes.

3. **ADD THE FILLING LAYER:** Sprinkle the crust evenly with the chocolate chips, pistachios, coconut, and dried cranberries. Drizzle with the sweetened condensed milk. Bake for 25 to 30 minutes, or until top turns golden. Cool completely.

4. **PREPARE THE SEMISWEET CHOCOLATE DRIZZLE:** Microwave the chocolate chips and shortening in a microwave-safe bowl on high for 30 seconds; remove and stir. Return to the microwave if not completely melted, and microwave in 15-second intervals until smooth and creamy. Do not overheat.

5. Drizzle the melted chocolate over the bars. Cut into 24 pieces.

rocky road brownie bars

YIELD 24 bars

PREP 20 minutes

BAKE 34 to 35 minutes

Signature Brownie recipe for 9 × 13-inch pan (page 19)

2 cups miniature marshmallows

1 cup (6 ounces) semisweet chocolate chips

1 cup (4 ounces) walnuts, chopped

Someone once described my rocky road brownies as the chocoholic highway to heaven—probably because of the extra helping of semisweet chocolate chips I add. These grab-and-go squares also have marshmallows (a childhood favorite) and walnuts (one of nature's super foods). It's this combination that makes these chewy, gooey, fudgy bars a favorite of all generations. Here's a suggestion: Bake a batch for your next road trip.

1. Preheat the oven to 350°F. Grease a 9 × 13-inch pan with butter or spray with nonstick cooking spray.

2. Prepare the signature brownie batter according to directions. Pour the batter into the prepared pan and bake for 30 minutes.

3. Sprinkle the marshmallows, chocolate chips, and nuts on top. Bake for an additional 4 to 5 minutes.

4. Cool completely and cut into 24 bars.

> Turn the pan halfway through the baking cycle so the marshmallows don't scorch.

toffee bars

YIELD   Approximately 20 irregular pieces

PREP   20 minutes

BAKE   25 minutes

SPECIAL EQUIPMENT

Jellyroll pan

hese toffee bars are terrific with a capital T. They're a lot like a Heath® bar, that American-made English toffee bar created by the Heath brothers in 1928. In this recipe, the brown sugar cookie batter provides a shortbread-like layer on the bottom with a crunchy toffee tier in the middle, and a swirl of melted semisweet chocolate chips on top. Premiere these on movie night, and you'll have a runaway hit on your hands.

COOKIE BATTER

1 cup light brown sugar, packed

1½ teaspoons pure vanilla extract

1 large egg

3 cups all-purpose flour

½ teaspoon salt

½ cup toffee bits (half of an 8-ounce bag)

TOFFEE LAYER

16 tablespoons (2 sticks) salted butter

1 cup light brown sugar, packed

1½ cups (9 ounces) semisweet chocolate chips

½ cup toffee bits (half of an 8-ounce bag)

1. Preheat the oven to 350°F. Grease a jellyroll pan with nonstick cooking spray or butter and set aside.

2. **PREPARE THE COOKIE BATTER:** Use an electric mixer set on the lowest speed or a spatula to mix the butter, brown sugar, and vanilla until creamy. Add the egg and mix thoroughly. Add the flour, salt, and toffee bits; mix thoroughly.

3. Scoop the cookie batter onto the prepared pan and press it into an even layer by hand. Bake for 14 to 16 minutes, until top is golden. Set aside, but leave the oven on.

4. **PREPARE THE TOFFEE LAYER:** Melt the butter and brown sugar in a saucepan over medium heat until bubbly. Continue heating and stirring for 2 to 3 minutes until caramelized. Pour the toffee over cookie crust and spread it evenly over the top. Bake for 8 minutes.

5. Remove the pan from the oven and sprinkle the top with the chocolate chips. Cover the pan with aluminum foil for 5 minutes, then remove the foil and swirl the melted chocolate chips with a spatula over top of toffee layer. Sprinkle with the toffee bits and chill in the refrigerator for 30 minutes.

6. To serve, break into irregular pieces, or cut into squares.

Heath® is a registered trademark of The Hershey Company

brownie cookies

My kids used to take a round cookie and nibble until they had a square. It was their way of making it last longer (and teasing me!). You won't have to go to those lengths with these, however, because they already come in different shapes and sizes. Some are shell shaped and dipped in chocolate, while others are oblong and designed for dunking. No matter how you eat these cookies, they're all sinfully delicious.

white chocolate shortbread thumbprint cookies

YIELD   18 cookies

PREP   25 minutes

BAKE   14 to 15 minutes

16 tablespoons (2 sticks) salted butter, softened

¾ cup sugar

1 teaspoon pure vanilla extract

2¼ cups all-purpose flour

¼ teaspoon salt

WHITE CHOCOLATE TOPPING

1 cup (6 ounces) white chocolate chips, or 3 dozen white chocolate melting discs

Coarse sea salt, for sprinkling

*B*een invited to a cookie swap? Forget slice-and-bake or store-bought. Bake and take these on a recyclable platter lined with lacy paper doilies. Then watch as other swappers fill their boxes with your cookies. They're downright delicious, lovely to look at, and evoke memories of childhood. Plus, they're so easy to make! Be sure to bring plenty of recipe cards to share.

1. Preheat the oven to 350°F.

2. Use an electric mixer to mix together the butter, sugar, and vanilla until creamy. Whisk together the flour and salt in a separate bowl. Add to the wet ingredients and mix thoroughly.

3. Roll the dough with your hands into 1-inch (1-ounce) balls and place on a nonstick baking sheet or a parchment paper-lined baking sheet. Use your thumb to create an indentation in the center of each cookie.

4. Bake for 14 to 15 minutes, or until the edges start to brown. Remove from the oven, fill the thumbprint in each cookie with white chocolate chips or melting discs, and sprinkle with sea salt. Store in an airtight container until ready to serve.

brownie biscotti

YIELD	36 biscotti
PREP	30 minutes
BAKE	40 to 50 minutes

8 tablespoons (1 stick) salted butter, softened

3 large eggs

2 teaspoons pure vanilla extract

2½ cups all-purpose flour

1¼ cups sugar

¾ cup 100% baking cocoa

1 teaspoon salt

½ teaspoon baking soda

1 cup (4 ounces) sliced almonds

1 cup (6 ounces) semisweet chocolate chips

Confectioners' sugar or melted white or semisweet chocolate chips with ¼ teaspoon vegetable shortening or coconut oil, for topping, optional

In Italian, biscotti means twice-baked. The English call them biscuits and Americans liken them to cookies. Because they are dry and originally made without eggs or oil, they enjoy a long shelf life. In fact, centuries ago, biscotti was a staple carried by the Roman legions.

Today, it's risen in status to become a gourmet-dunking cookie in coffeehouses everywhere. Most recipes now include eggs, and the flavor variations are limited only by your imagination. Of course, my imagination led me straight to brownie biscotti. Bake them twice, brew a pot of coffee, put your feet up, and start dunking.

1. Preheat the oven to 350°F.

2. Use an electric mixer or spatula to mix together the butter, eggs, and vanilla until well blended. Whisk together the flour, sugar, cocoa, salt, and baking soda in a separate bowl. Add the dry ingredients to the wet ingredients gradually until thoroughly mixed and a dough forms. Turn the dough onto a floured surface. Add the almonds and chocolate chips and mix them into the dough by hand.

3. Divide dough in half and place both halves on an ungreased baking sheet. Form each half into a log, approximately 12 inches long, keeping the width uniform in size.

4. Bake the logs for 30 to 35 minutes, until firm. Allow to cool for 15 minutes.

5. Transfer to a cutting board and slice into ½-inch portions. Return to the baking sheet with the cut sides down. Bake for 10 to 15 minutes, until dry. Allow to cool on wire racks.

6. Serve unadorned, or dust the biscotti with confectioners' sugar or drizzle with melted white or semisweet chocolate, if you like. To prepare the chocolate drizzle, microwave the white or semisweet chocolate chips and shortening in microwave-safe bowl on high for 30 seconds; remove and stir. Return to the microwave if not thoroughly melted, and microwave in 15-second intervals until smooth and creamy. (Do not overheat or the chocolate will scorch.)

brownie buckeye cookies

YIELD 15 cookies

PREP 25 minutes

BAKE 11 minutes

SPECIAL EQUIPMENT
Large and small scoops

BROWNIE COOKIES

2 cups (12 ounces) semisweet chocolate chips

6 tablespoons salted butter

2 large eggs

1 teaspoon pure vanilla extract

½ cup sugar

1 cup all-purpose flour

½ teaspoon baking powder

¼ teaspoon salt

1 tablespoon 100% baking cocoa

PEANUT BUTTER FILLING

1 cup creamy peanut butter (all-natural recommended)

1 cup confectioners' sugar

SEMISWEET CHOCOLATE TOPPING

½ cup (3 ounces) semisweet chocolate chips

¼ teaspoon vegetable shortening or coconut oil

W *hat's not to like about buckeyes—those small peanut butter balls surrounded by creamy milk chocolate? I'll tell you: They're labor intensive! So, one holiday season, when my to-do list outdistanced my time, I decided to create something quick and easy with the same terrific taste. These cookies take half as long to make as buckeyes, are less messy to eat, and deliver the same peanut buttery chocolate taste we all know and love. That first Christmas, no one even missed the buckeyes, and I had a few precious moments to myself to relax. P.S. I haven't made traditional buckeyes since.*

1. Preheat the oven to 350°F. Grease a sheet pan and set aside.

2. PREPARE THE BROWNIE COOKIES: Microwave chocolate chips and butter in microwave-safe bowl on high for 30 seconds; remove and stir. Return to the microwave if not thoroughly melted, and microwave in 15-second intervals until smooth and creamy.

3. Use an electric mixer set on the lowest speed or spatula to mix together the eggs, vanilla, and sugar in a separate bowl. Blend the egg mixture into the melted chocolate mixture. Add the flour, baking powder, salt, and cocoa, and mix thoroughly.

4. Use a large scoop to measure portions of the batter onto the prepared sheet pan. Bake for 11 minutes, or until center is set and edges begin to crisp. Allow to cool completely.

5. PREPARE THE PEANUT BUTTER FILLING: Mix together the peanut butter and confectioners' sugar. Mix until blended.

6. Use a small scoop to measure portions of the peanut butter filling and roll them into small balls by hand. Press a ball of the peanut butter filling into the center of each brownie cookie.

7. PREPARE THE SEMISWEET CHOCOLATE TOPPING: Microwave the chocolate chips and shortening as per step 2.

8. Scoop a tablespoon of the melted chocolate topping onto the center of the peanut butter mixture. Let cool for 15 minutes to allow the chocolate to set.

brownie whoopie pies

YIELD 22 mini (1½-inch) whoopie pies

PREP 25 minutes

BAKE 11 minutes

SPECIAL EQUIPMENT

Macaroon pan with 1¾-inch molds; stand mixer with whisk attachment

WHOOPIE PIE BROWNIES

2 cups (12 ounces) semisweet chocolate chips

6 tablespoons salted butter

½ cup sugar

2 large eggs

1 teaspoon pure vanilla extract

¾ cup all-purpose flour

½ teaspoon baking powder

¼ teaspoon salt

1 tablespoon 100% baking cocoa

CREAM CHEESE FILLING

1 (8-ounce) package of cream cheese, at room temperature

1 cup confectioners' sugar

4 tablespoons (½ stick) salted butter, softened

1 teaspoon pure vanilla extract

Typically, a whoopie pie is two round pieces of chocolate sponge cake filled with vanilla frosting. At one time, they were indispensable when it came to packing lunchboxes. As my kids got older and their palates became more refined (just kidding!), I thought why not make whoopie pies at home—out of brownies!

So one rainy day, we mixed up a batch of my Signature Brownie batter (the only adjustments were an extra ¼ cup of flour and reduced baking time). While the kids were dropping batter for the tops and bottoms into a macaroon pan, I whipped up a fluffy cream cheese filling (which everyone agreed was way tastier than old boring vanilla frosting). Assembling the whoopie pies was a hoot, and my little bakers, while a bit sticky, were proud they had helped create a new family dessert.

1. Preheat the oven to 350°F. Grease a macaroon pan with nonstick cooking spray and set aside.

2. PREPARE THE WHOOPIE PIE BROWNIES: Microwave the chocolate chips and butter in a microwave-safe bowl on high for 30 seconds; remove and stir. Return to the microwave if not thoroughly melted, and microwave in 15-second intervals until smooth and creamy.

3. Use an electric mixer set on the lowest speed or a spatula to mix the sugar, eggs, and vanilla in a separate bowl. Blend the egg mixture into the melted chocolate mixture until well combined. Add the flour, baking powder, salt, and cocoa and mix until thoroughly combined.

4. Drop 1 tablespoon of the batter into each cavity of the prepared macaroon pan. Bake for 11 minutes, or until centers are set and edges begin to crisp. Cool completely.

5. PREPARE CREAM CHEESE FILLING: Use a stand mixer with a whisk attachment to beat the cream cheese, confectioners' sugar, butter, and vanilla on medium speed until smooth and fluffy, 2 to 3 minutes.

6. Scoop approximately ½ tablespoon of the filling with tip of a spoon and place it on the flat side of a whoopie pie brownie. Place the flat side of another whoopie pie brownie on top of the filling to create a sandwich. Repeat with the remaining whoopie pie brownies and filling. Store in an airtight container for up to 1 week in the refrigerator.

cookies and cream brownie cookies

YIELD: 22 cookies

PREP 35 minutes

BAKE 8 minutes

SPECIAL EQUIPMENT

Small scoop; pastry bag with assorted tips (nice, but not required)

The cookies and cream craze has overtaken the dessert world, winding its way into ice cream, fudge, cupcakes, you name it. Why not cookies and cream brownie cookies? And why not stack them like a sandwich, which was my granddaughter, Juliana's, idea. "Oh, and grandma, can you put some vanilla frosting in the middle?" I'm pretty sure this was her way of charming me out of two cookies at one time. Whatever her reasoning, she was spot-on. (Maybe she inherited my "baking" gene.) These chewy, buttery double-deckers are a real sweet treat. Just add a glass of milk.

BROWNIE COOKIE BATTER

2 cups (12 ounces) semisweet chocolate chips

6 tablespoons salted butter

2 large eggs

½ cup sugar

1 teaspoon pure vanilla extract

1 cup all-purpose flour

½ teaspoon baking powder

¼ teaspoon salt

1 tablespoon 100% baking cocoa

VANILLA FROSTING

¼ cup salted butter, softened

¼ cup vegetable shortening or coconut oil

2 cups confectioners' sugar

1½ teaspoons pure vanilla extract

1. Preheat the oven to 350°F. Grease a sheet pan and set aside.

2. **PREPARE THE BROWNIE COOKIE BATTER:** Microwave the chocolate chips and butter in a microwave-safe bowl on high for 30 seconds; remove and stir. Return to the microwave if not thoroughly melted, and microwave in 15-second intervals until smooth and creamy. (Do not overheat or the chocolate will scorch.)

3. Use an electric mixer or spatula to mix the eggs, sugar, and vanilla in a separate bowl until well combined. Blend the egg mixture into the melted chocolate mixture. Add the flour, baking powder, salt, and cocoa and mix until thoroughly combined.

4. Use a small scoop to measure out a portion of batter to check the consistency. If batter is too soft to hold its shape, let stand for 15 to 20 minutes until firm. When the dough is firm, measure out scoops of batter and form each scoop into a ball by hand; place them on the prepared baking sheet.

5. Bake for 8 minutes, until edges begin to crisp. Allow cookies to cool completely.

6. **PREPARE THE VANILLA FROSTING:** Use an electric mixer to mix the butter and shortening together on low speed until well blended. Add the confectioners' sugar and vanilla gradually and beat on high for 2 minutes until thoroughly mixed.

7. Turn the cooled cookies flat side up. Fill a pastry bag with frosting, if desired. Using a pastry bag or a spoon, top half of the cookies with the icing and place the rest of the cookies on top, flat side down, to create cookie sandwiches. Store in an airtight container for up to 1 week.

hazelnut cookies

1 cup (4 ounces) hazelnuts, chopped

2 cups (12 ounces) semisweet chocolate chips

6 tablespoons salted butter

2 large eggs

¾ cup sugar

1 teaspoon pure vanilla extract

½ cup all-purpose flour

½ teaspoon baking powder

¼ teaspoon salt

1 tablespoon 100% baking cocoa

1½ cups (9 ounces) white chocolate chips

Chocolate and hazelnuts are made for each other. Just ask the French (the Italians, Germans, or Swiss). Their patisseries and bakeries are brimming with biscotti, pies, tarts, and tortes flavored with these superbly compatible ingredients. Here's my way of uniting these two Old World flavors with an all-American favorite: chocolate chip cookies.

1. Preheat the oven to 350°F. Grease a cookie sheet and set aside.

2. Toast the hazelnuts on a baking sheet in a single layer for 5 to 7 minutes or until golden. Remove from the oven and set aside.

3. Microwave the chocolate chips and butter in a microwave-safe bowl on high for 30 seconds; remove and stir. Return to the microwave if not thoroughly melted, and microwave in 15-second intervals until smooth and creamy. (Do not overheat or the chocolate will scorch.)

4. Use an electric mixer or a spatula to mix the eggs, sugar, and vanilla in a separate bowl. Blend the egg mixture into the melted chocolate mixture.

5. Whisk together the flour, baking powder, salt, cocoa, white chocolate chips, and toasted hazelnuts. Add the wet ingredients to the dry ingredients and mix thoroughly.

6. Use a small scoop to measure portions of the batter and place them on the prepared cookie sheet, leaving approximately 2 inches between each cookie. Bake for 12 to 14 minutes, until edges begin to crisp. Remove the cookies from the cookie sheet when the pan is warm to the touch.

> Turn a simple scoop of ice cream into a decadent dessert by accompanying it with just one of these delectable cookies.

black and white brownie cookies

YIELD   12 cookies

PREP   20 minutes

BAKE   11 minutes

SPECIAL EQUIPMENT

Large scoop

BROWNIE COOKIES

2 cups (12 ounces) semisweet chocolate chips

6 tablespoons salted butter

2 large eggs

1 teaspoon pure vanilla extract

½ cup sugar

1 cup all-purpose flour

½ teaspoon baking powder

¼ teaspoon salt

1 tablespoon 100% baking cocoa

ICING

⅓ cup (2 ounces) chopped unsweetened chocolate

½ cup water, plus more hot water if needed

¼ cup light corn syrup

6 cups confectioners' sugar

½ teaspoon pure vanilla extract

I grew up in Syracuse, New York, and one of my fondest childhood memories is of getting up Sunday morning and going to Snowflake Bakery with my father. Our mission: to pick up rolls and pastries for brunch. Of all the sweets in the pastry case, the black and white cookies—or half-and-halfs, as they are sometimes called— were my favorite. (I know this is hard to believe, but I liked the vanilla side better!)

Although it's difficult to improve upon perfection, for this recipe, I decided to replace the traditional shortbread bottom with a fudgy brownie base. I didn't tinker with the chocolate and vanilla icing, however. To this day, every time I make these, it takes me home to Syracuse and Sundays with my dad.

1. Preheat the oven to 350°F. Grease a sheet pan and set aside.

2. **PREPARE THE BROWNIE COOKIES:** Microwave the chocolate chips and butter in a microwave-safe bowl on high for 30 seconds; remove and stir. Return to the microwave if not thoroughly melted, and microwave in 15-second intervals until smooth and creamy.

3. Use an electric mixer or a spatula to mix the eggs, vanilla, and sugar in a separate bowl. Blend the egg mixture into the melted chocolate mixture until well combined. Whisk together the flour, baking powder, salt, and cocoa in a separate bowl. Add the dry ingredients to the wet ingredients and mix thoroughly.

4. Use a large scoop to measure out portions of the batter and drop them onto the prepared sheet pan. Bake for 11 minutes, until edges begin to crisp and centers are firm. Allow to cool.

5. **PREPARE THE ICING:** Microwave the chocolate in a microwave-safe bowl on high in 15-second increments until smooth and creamy. Set aside.

6. Bring the water and corn syrup to a boil in a medium saucepan. Remove from the heat and stir in the confectioners' sugar and vanilla. The icing should be slightly runny; add additional hot water if too thick.

7. Transfer half of the white icing to a bowl. Turn the cookies flat side up. Drop a tablespoon of white icing on one half of each cookie. Use a spatula or butter knife to spread it evenly.

8. Add the remaining white icing to the melted chocolate and blend thoroughly. Spread a tablespoon of chocolate icing on the other half of each cookie.

9. Let stand until the icing is set. Store in a single layer in an airtight container for up to 2 weeks in the refrigerator or 1 week at room temperature.

brownie haystacks

YIELD   Approximately 40 haystacks

PREP   20 minutes

BAKE   8 to 10 minutes

SPECIAL EQUIPMENT
     Small scoop

Remember haystacks? Those chocolate-covered coconut candies that resembled tiny haystacks that were often found in boxes of assorted chocolates way back when. If you liked them, you'll love these irregular lumps of chocolate and coconut perfection. They're rich, chewy, and the chocolate drizzle finds its way into every nook and cranny. It's practically impossible to eat just one.

2 cups (12 ounces) semisweet chocolate chips

6 tablespoons salted butter

2 large eggs

½ cup sugar

1 teaspoon pure vanilla extract

¾ cup all-purpose flour

½ teaspoon baking powder

¼ teaspoon salt

1 tablespoon 100% baking cocoa

3½ cups sweetened flaked coconut

1 teaspoon pure almond extract

SEMISWEET CHOCOLATE DRIZZLE

½ cup (3 ounces) semisweet chocolate chips

¼ teaspoon vegetable shortening or coconut oil

1. Preheat the oven to 350°F. Grease a sheet pan with butter or nonstick cooking spray and set aside.

2. Microwave the chocolate chips and butter in a microwave-safe bowl on high for 30 seconds; remove and stir. Return to the microwave if not thoroughly melted, and microwave in 15-second intervals until smooth and creamy. (Do not overheat or the chocolate will scorch.)

3. Use an electric mixer or a spatula to mix together the eggs, sugar, and vanilla until well combined. Pour the egg mixture into the melted chocolate and mix until well combined. Whisk together the flour, baking powder, salt, and cocoa in a separate bowl until blended. Add the dry ingredients to the wet ingredients and mix thoroughly.

4. Mix the coconut and almond extract. Add the coconut mixture to the brownie batter and mix with a spatula.

5. Use a small scoop to measure portions of the batter and drop them onto the prepared baking sheet. Bake for 8 to 10 minutes, until toothpick inserted in center comes out clean. Pinch the tops while still warm to form peaks. Allow to cool.

6. **PREPARE THE SEMISWEET CHOCOLATE DRIZZLE**: Microwave the chocolate chips and shortening in a microwave-safe bowl on high for 30 seconds; remove and stir. Return to the microwave if not thoroughly melted, and microwave in 15-second intervals until smooth and creamy. (Do not overheat or the chocolate will scorch.)

7. Drizzle the melted chocolate over the cooled haystacks.

chocolate-dipped brownie madeleines

YIELD 28 cookies

PREP 20 minutes

BAKE 10 to 12 minutes per batch

SPECIAL EQUIPMENT
Madeleine pan; small scoop

I f you ever tackle Marcel Proust's In Search of Lost Time, you'll find the delicate shell-shaped madeleine plays a significant role in the novel's theme of involuntary memory. But, rather than have a madeleine for a muse, I'm more interested in baking one that's unforgettable. So, mine is chocolate through and through, which is decidedly more decadent than the French version.

MADELEINE BATTER

2 cups (12 ounces) semisweet chocolate chips

6 tablespoons salted butter

2 large eggs

1 teaspoon pure vanilla extract

½ cup sugar

¾ cup all-purpose flour

½ teaspoon baking powder

¼ teaspoon salt

1 tablespoon 100% baking cocoa

DARK CHOCOLATE DIP

2 cups (12 ounces) dark chocolate chips

½ teaspoon vegetable shortening or coconut oil

Coarse sea salt, chocolate sprinkles, or chopped nuts, for topping

1. Preheat the oven to 350°F.

2. **PREPARE THE MADELEINE BATTER:** Microwave the chocolate chips and butter in a microwave-safe bowl on high for 30 seconds; remove and stir. Return to the microwave if not thoroughly melted, and microwave in 15-second intervals until smooth and creamy. (Do not overheat or the chocolate will scorch.)

3. Use an electric mixer or spatula to mix the eggs, vanilla, and sugar in a separate bowl. Blend the egg mixture into the melted chocolate mixture. Add the flour, baking powder, salt, and cocoa and mix thoroughly.

4. Grease the madeleine pan with nonstick cooking spray. Use a small scoop to measure portions of the batter and fill each cavity of the prepared pan. Bake for 10 to 12 minutes, until edges begin to crisp. Set aside to cool, then fill the molds with the remaining batter and bake.

5. **PREPARE THE DARK CHOCOLATE DIP:** Microwave the chocolate chips and shortening in a microwave-safe bowl on high for 30 seconds; remove and stir. Return to the microwave if not thoroughly melted, and microwave in 15-second intervals until smooth. (Do not overheat or the chocolate will scorch.)

6. Dip one-third of each madeleine in the melted chocolate. Sprinkle the melted chocolate tips with sea salt, chocolate sprinkles, or chopped nuts. Place on a piece of parchment paper until the chocolate has set. Store in an airtight container until ready to serve.

blonde bombshells

YIELD   38 blonde madeleines

PREP   20 minutes

BAKE   10 to 12 minutes per batch

SPECIAL EQUIPMENT

Madeleine pan; small scoop

Even in her heyday back in the '50's, film star Brigitte Bardot, a blonde bombshell in her own right, couldn't hold a candle to this cross between a blonde brownie and the small French butter cake known as a madeleine. The ideal accompaniment to a cup of tea at the end of a long day, these treats are also special enough to serve at a fancy dinner party.

12 tablespoons (1½ sticks) salted butter, melted

1½ cups light brown sugar, packed

2 eggs

2 teaspoons pure vanilla extract

1¾ cups all-purpose flour

1 teaspoon baking powder

½ teaspoon salt

1 cup (6 ounces) chocolate chips, white chocolate chips, or combination

Confectioners' sugar, for dusting

1. Preheat the oven to 325°F. Spray a madeleine pan with nonstick cooking spray and set aside.

2. Use an electric mixer or a spatula to mix together the melted butter and brown sugar thoroughly. Add the eggs and vanilla and mix well. Add the flour, baking powder, and salt and mix thoroughly. Use a spatula to fold the chocolate chips into the batter until evenly distributed. Allow the batter to sit at room temperature for 10 to 15 minutes to firm up.

3. Use a small scoop to deposit a scoop of batter into each section of the prepared madeleine pan. Bake for 10 to 12 minutes, until edges begin to crisp.

4. Cool completely in the pan and then remove the blonde bombshells from the molds and dust the tops with confectioners' sugar. Spray the madeleine pan with nonstick spray again, and repeat until you have used up all the batter.

brownie in a pie shell

The recipes in this chapter really get around, from New York Cheesecake to Kentucky Pecan Pie. And while their origins may differ, they all have one thing in common: a nontraditional crunchy, buttery, chocolate crust. Looking for something special? Any one of these pies takes the cake.

praline cheesecake with brownie brittle™ crust

YIELD 8 to 10 slices

PREP 25 minutes

BAKE 45 to 50 minutes

SPECIAL EQUIPMENT
9-inch loose-bottom or springform pan

BROWNIE BRITTLE™ CRUST

1 cup BROWNIE BRITTLE™
(one 5-ounce bag = 1 cup crushed)
or chocolate wafers crushed in
a food processor

4 tablespoons salted butter, melted

PRALINE CHEESECAKE

1½ pounds bulk cream cheese
or 3 (8-ounce) packages, at
room temperature

1¼ cups dark brown sugar, packed

2 tablespoons all-purpose flour

3 large eggs

1½ teaspoons pure vanilla extract

½ cup (2 ounces) pecans, finely
chopped, plus more whole or half
pecans for garnish

Maple syrup, for brushing

My sister, Judi, deserves most of the credit for this masterpiece. (My contribution was switching out the traditional graham-cracker crust for one made from chocolate chip BROWNIE BRITTLE™.) The filling is firm yet creamy with hints of vanilla and pecans. For a festive finishing touch, brush the cooled cheesecake with maple syrup and strategically place pecan halves on top—around the edge, in the middle, in a heart shape—whatever strikes your fancy. If you want a dessert that elicits oohs and ahs from family and friends, this cheesecake delivers.

1. Preheat the oven to 350°F.

2. Mix the crushed BROWNIE BRITTLE™ with the melted butter and press into the bottom of a 9-inch loose-bottom pan. Bake for 10 minutes and set aside to cool. Increase the oven temperature to 450°F.

3. Using a food processor, beat the cream cheese until soft and creamy. Add the brown sugar and flour and mix until well blended. Beat in the eggs, one at a time, and the vanilla until the filling is smooth and creamy. Stir in the nuts and pour the filling into the crust.

4. Bake for 10 minutes. Reduce the oven temperature to 250°F and continue baking for 25 to 30 minutes, or until the center looks almost set. Turn the oven off; leave the cake inside the oven for 5 minutes.

5. Run a knife around the sides of the pan to loosen the cheesecake, but allow it to cool on a wire rack before removing the rim. Chill until serving time.

6. Just before serving, brush the top of the cheesecake with maple syrup and garnish with pecans.

new york cheesecake with brownie brittle™ crust

YIELD	8 to 10 servings
PREP	25 minutes
BAKE	48 to 50 minutes
SPECIAL EQUIPMENT	
	9-inch loose-bottom or springform pan

BROWNIE BRITTLE™ CRUST

1 cup BROWNIE BRITTLE™
(one 5-ounce bag = 1 cup crushed)
or chocolate wafers crushed in
a food processor

3 tablespoons sugar

3 tablespoons salted butter, melted

CHEESECAKE FILLING

3 (8-ounce) packages cream
cheese, softened

1 cup sugar

3 tablespoons all-purpose flour

2 tablespoons fresh lemon juice

1 teaspoon pure vanilla extract

3 large eggs plus 1 egg white

With Greek yogurt all the rage these days, you probably won't be surprised to learn that the earliest version of cheesecake came from Greece. It contained just three ingredients: cheese, flour, and honey. While classic New York cheesecake has a few more ingredients, it's still served the Greek way—solo. No fruit, sauces, caramel, or chocolate to keep it company. So here was my dilemma: How do I stay faithful to a tradition that's survived thousands of years and still get chocolate in there? My twenty-first-century solution: Make the crust with butter and chocolate! And there you have it—a minor modification that gives this classic recipe a brownie-lover's makeover.

1. Preheat the oven to 350°F. Grease a 9-inch loose-bottom pan and set aside.

2. **PREPARE THE BROWNIE BRITTLE™ CRUST:** Mix together the crushed BROWNIE BRITTLE™, sugar, and melted butter. Pat the crumb mixture firmly and evenly into the bottom of the prepared pan. Bake for 8 to 10 minutes, and set aside to cool. Increase the oven temperature to 450°F.

3. **PREPARE THE CHEESECAKE FILLING:** Combine the cream cheese, sugar, flour, lemon juice, and vanilla in a food processor and mix on medium speed until well blended. Add the eggs, one at a time, mixing well after each addition. Mix in the egg white until well blended.

4. Pour the cheesecake filling onto the crust and bake for 10 minutes. Reduce the oven temperature to 250°F and continue baking for 30 minutes, until center is set and edges begin to pull away from sides of pan.

5. Run a knife around the sides of the pan to loosen it, but allow the cheesecake to cool on a wire rack before removing the rim. Chill until serving time.

peppermint pie with brownie brittle crust

YIELD	8 to 10 servings
PREP	15 minutes
BAKE	8 minutes

BROWNIE BRITTLE™ CRUST

2 cups BROWNIE BRITTLE™
(one 5-ounce bag = 1 cup crushed)
or chocolate wafers crushed in
a food processor

6 tablespoons salted butter, melted

FLUFFY PEPPERMINT FILLING

8 ounces hard peppermint candy
(sticks are best), plus more for
garnish (optional)

½ cup half-and-half

Half a ¼-ounce envelope
unflavored gelatin

2 tablespoons cold water

1 (8-ounce) container frozen whipped
topping, thawed

Restaurant managers who strategically place a bowl of peppermints near the exit are onto something. They know nothing cleanses the palate and soothes digestion faster than a hint of mint. (Plus, it leaves patrons with a sweet impression of their dining experience.) This light, refreshing pie does the same, with one slight improvement: It rests the creamy, fluffy, minty filling on a crunchy, buttery, chocolate crust. (And we all know there's no happier combination than mint and chocolate.) This is the ideal dessert to nibble on after a huge holiday dinner.

1. Preheat the oven to 350°F.

2. **PREPARE THE BROWNIE BRITTLE™ CRUST:** Mix the crushed BROWNIE BRITTLE™ with the melted butter. Press the crumb mixture into the bottom and sides of a 9-inch pie pan. Bake for 8 minutes and set aside to cool.

3. **PREPARE THE FLUFFY PEPPERMINT FILLING:** Crush the peppermint candy and put it in a microwave-safe bowl. Add the half-and-half and microwave it on high for 30 seconds, or until the candy melts. Mix together the gelatin and cold water, and then stir it into the melted candy mixture. Chill until almost set.

4. Use a spatula to fold the whipped topping into the chilled candy mixture, then pour the filling over the crust. Chill until serving time.

5. Garnish with crushed peppermint candies before serving, if you like.

pumpkin pie with brownie brittle crust

YIELD	8 to 10 servings
PREP	15 minutes
BAKE	50 minutes

This recent addition to our family's holiday fare was a H-U-G-E hit! It's spicy, sweet flavor and rich, creamy texture are what you'd expect from a much more complicated recipe. But it really is a breeze to make. Guess you could say it's as easy as pie. And who doesn't appreciate easy around the holidays? Or, pie for that matter!

BROWNIE BRITTLE™ CRUST

1½ cups BROWNIE BRITTLE™
(one 5-ounce bag = 1 cup crushed)
or chocolate wafers crushed in
a food processor

6 tablespoons salted butter, melted

PUMPKIN FILLING

1 (15-ounce) can pureed pumpkin

¼ teaspoon ground cloves

½ teaspoon ground ginger

½ teaspoon ground nutmeg

1 teaspoon ground cinnamon

¼ teaspoon salt

2 large eggs

1 (14-ounce) can sweetened
condensed milk

1. Preheat the oven to 350°F.

2. **PREPARE THE BROWNIE BRITTLE™ CRUST:** Mix the crushed BROWNIE BRITTLE™ with the melted butter. Press the crumb mixture firmly and evenly into the bottom and sides of a 9-inch pie pan. Bake for 10 minutes and set aside to cool. Increase the oven temperature to 425°F.

3. **PREPARE THE PUMPKIN FILLING:** Combine the pumpkin, cloves, ginger, nutmeg, cinnamon, and salt in a small saucepan. Stir and cook over low heat for 5 minutes to allow the flavors to meld. Set aside and allow to cool.

4. Beat the eggs thoroughly in a bowl and then mix in the sweetened condensed milk. Add the cooled pumpkin and spice mixture to the egg mixture and blend thoroughly.

5. Pour the pumpkin filling into the crust and bake for 15 minutes.

6. Reduce the oven temperature to 350°F and bake an additional 35 minutes or until center appears to be set.

7. Allow the pie to cool completely, then refrigerate until ready to serve.

chocolate-almond brownie tart

YIELD 12 servings

PREP 20 minutes

BAKE 8 minutes

SPECIAL EQUIPMENT
11-inch tart pan

BROWNIE BRITTLE™ CRUST

2½ cups BROWNIE BRITTLE™
(one 5-ounce bag = 1 cup crushed)
or chocolate wafers crushed in
a food processor

10 tablespoons (1 stick plus 2
tablespoons) salted butter, melted

CHOCOLATE ALMOND FILLING

1½ cups slivered almonds

2⅔ cups (16 ounces) semisweet
chocolate chips

1 cup heavy cream

1 teaspoon pure almond extract

*H*ere's a dessert everyone in my circle is nuts about. That's because the taste of almonds infuses every bite. For starters, the crunchy BROWNIE BRITTLE™ crust, made with plenty of creamy butter, is topped with toasted almonds. (Truly a most pleasant surprise!) Almond extract enhances the filling. And slivered almonds decorate the top. Simple ingredients. Easy prep. Perfect to prepare ahead of time. This is about as fuss-free as a dessert gets.

1. Preheat the oven to 350°F. Grease an 11-inch tart pan with nonstick cooking spray.

2. **PREPARE THE BROWNIE BRITTLE™ CRUST:** Mix together the crushed BROWNIE BRITTLE™ and melted butter until well combined. Press the crumb mixture firmly and evenly into the bottom and sides of the prepared tart pan. Bake for 8 minutes, then set aside to cool. Leave the oven on.

3. **PREPARE THE CHOCOLATE ALMOND FILLING:** Arrange the almond slivers in a single layer on an ungreased baking sheet and toast in the oven until slightly golden, about 10 minutes. Check every minute or two, turning the almonds often to make sure they toast evenly and do not burn. Sprinkle the toasted almonds evenly over the crust, reserving ¼ cup for garnish. Turn the oven off.

4. Microwave the chocolate chips in a microwave-safe bowl on high for 30 seconds; remove and stir. Return to the microwave if not completely melted, and microwave in 15-second intervals until smooth. (Do not overheat or the chocolate will scorch.)

5. Heat the heavy cream in a small saucepan only until warmed through. Pour the warm cream over the melted chocolate and blend until smooth and creamy. Add the almond extract and mix thoroughly.

6. Pour the chocolate mixture over the toasted almond-covered crust. Sprinkle the top of the tart with the remaining ¼ cup almond slivers.

7. Chill in the refrigerator for 1 to 2 hours before slicing and serving.

kentucky pecan and chocolate pie

YIELD	8 to 10 servings
PREP	25 minutes
BAKE	1 hour 10 minutes

BROWNIE BRITTLE™ CRUST

2 cups BROWNIE BRITTLE™
(one 5-ounce bag = 1 cup crushed)
or chocolate wafers crushed in
a food processor

6 tablespoons salted butter, melted

BOURBON PECAN FILLING

1 cup corn syrup

1 cup dark brown sugar, packed

¼ teaspoon salt

6 tablespoons salted butter, melted

1 teaspoon pure vanilla extract

2 tablespoons bourbon

4 large eggs, beaten

1½ cups (6 ounces) chopped pecans

½ cup (3 ounces) semisweet
chocolate chips

W hat singular ingredient gives this Southern charmer its character? Is it the brown sugar, butter, or pecans? Although each of these contributes to the pie's yumminess quotient, every pecan pie worth its salt has this trio in it. You might think it's the nontraditional chocolate crust, and if you were a true chocoholic, you would be right, but what really kicks this recipe up a notch is the spike of bourbon. Warning: Be sure to clear a path to the table, because I guarantee the adults will race for a slice of this pie.

1. Preheat the oven to 350°F.

2. **PREPARE THE BROWNIE BRITTLE™ CRUST:** Mix the crushed BROWNIE BRITTLE™ with the melted butter. Press the crumb mixture firmly and evenly into the bottom and sides of a 9-inch pie pan. Bake for 8 to 10 minutes and set aside to cool.

3. **PREPARE THE BOURBON PECAN FILLING:** Use an electric mixer or a spatula to mix together the corn syrup, brown sugar, salt, butter, vanilla, and bourbon until thoroughly combined. Add the eggs and beat well to combine. Stir in the pecans and chocolate chips.

4. Pour the filling into the crust and bake for 30 minutes; loosely cover the top of the pie with aluminum foil and continue baking another 30 minutes, until center is set. Let cool before slicing and serving.

deliciously round brownies

Cake pops. Truffles. Bonbons. These circular confections satisfy butter-chocolate cravings whether they're perched on skewers or lollipop sticks, or nestled in decorative baker's cups. These are my go-to recipes whenever fun is on the menu.

candy apple brownie cake pops

*C*ake on a stick? What a concept! In my family, the only thing better, of course, is brownies on a stick. While many recipes take a shortcut and use a boxed cake mix, I prefer to make my brownie cake pops from scratch. The contrast between the deep chocolate brownie and the bright red candy coating is what makes these cake pops POP!

CAKE POP BATTER

2 cups (12 ounces) semisweet chocolate chips

6 tablespoons salted butter

2 large eggs

1 teaspoon pure vanilla extract

½ cup sugar

¾ cup all-purpose flour

½ teaspoon baking powder

¼ teaspoon salt

1 tablespoon 100% baking cocoa

CANDY APPLE COATING

2 cups sugar

¾ cup water

½ cup light corn syrup

½ teaspoon liquid red food coloring

1 cup red sanding sugar, for garnish, optional

1. Preheat the oven to 350°F. Grease an 8 × 8-inch pan and set aside.

2. PREPARE THE CAKE POP BATTER: Microwave the chocolate chips and butter in a large microwave-safe bowl on high for 30 seconds; remove and stir. Return to microwave if not completely melted, and microwave in 15-second intervals until smooth and creamy. (Do not overheat or the chocolate will scorch.)

3. Mix together the eggs, vanilla, and sugar in a separate bowl, until well combined. Stir the egg mixture into the melted chocolate mixture. Add the flour, baking powder, salt, and cocoa and mix thoroughly.

4. Spoon the batter into the prepared pan and bake for 25 minutes. Set aside to cool. Repeat with the remaining batter, if necessary.

5. Trim the edges away from the cooled cake. Use an electric mixer or food processor to mix the cake thoroughly until the consistency is pliable enough to form small balls.

6. Use a small scoop to measure out a portion of batter and roll it into a ball by hand. Repeat with the remainder of the batter.

7. Insert a cake pop stick into the center of each ball and freeze the cake pops for 30 minutes.

8. PREPARE THE CANDY APPLE COATING: Mix together the sugar, water, corn syrup, and red food coloring. Dip the chilled brownie cake pops into the candy apple mixture.

9. Sprinkle the red sanding sugar into a shallow dish and roll each cake pop in the sugar to evenly coat. Display the finished cake pops in a stand, tall drinking glass, or foam block. Chill in the refrigerator until ready to serve.

strawberry blonde cake pops

YIELD   32 cake pops

PREP   20 minutes

BAKE   25 minutes

SPECIAL EQUIPMENT

   Cake pop sticks; small scoop

STRAWBERRY BLONDE CAKE POPS

12 tablespoons (1½ sticks) salted butter, melted

1½ cups sugar

2 large eggs

2 teaspoons pure vanilla extract

1½ cups all-purpose flour

1 teaspoon baking powder

½ teaspoon salt

1 cup strawberry preserves

WHITE OR SEMISWEET CHOCOLATE COATING

2 cups (12 ounces) white chocolate chips or semisweet chocolate chips

½ teaspoon vegetable shortening or coconut oil

If only Marie Antoinette had said, "Let them eat cake pops," perhaps this last queen of France might have survived the Revolution. I mean no one can stay angry with you when you serve these priceless little gems: They're filled with strawberry preserves and coated with your choice of chocolate. Even though they seem extravagant, they're actually made from the most common ingredients: sugar, eggs, flour. Yet, they're fit for royalty.

1. Preheat the oven to 325°F. Grease a 9 × 13-inch pan and set aside.

2. PREPARE THE STRAWBERRY BLONDE CAKE POPS: Use an electric mixer or a spatula to mix together the melted butter and sugar until well combined. Blend in the eggs and vanilla. Add the flour, baking powder, and salt and mix thoroughly.

3. Spread the batter into the prepared pan. Bake for 25 minutes until slightly underbaked, and set aside to cool.

4. Remove the brownie from the pan and trim away the crisp edges. Place the brownie in a food processor and process for 2 minutes, until pliable (if the batter is too soft, refrigerate it).

5. Fill half of a small scoop with batter, then add a dollop of strawberry preserves in the center. Fill the remainder of the scoop with more batter and roll it into a ball using your hands. Insert a cake pop stick into the center and set aside. Repeat with the remaining batter and preserves. Chill the cake pops in the refrigerator for 30 minutes.

6. PREPARE THE CHOCOLATE COATING: Microwave the chocolate chips and shortening in a microwave-safe bowl on high for 30 seconds; remove and stir. Return to the microwave if not thoroughly melted, and microwave in 15-second intervals until smooth and creamy. (Do not overheat or the chocolate will scorch.)

7. Dip the chilled cake pops into the melted chocolate to evenly coat. Put the cake pops in a stand, tall drinking glass, or foam block until the coating has set. Store them in a cool dry place until ready to serve.

macaroon cake pops

YIELD   16 cake pops

PREP   25 to 30 minutes

BAKE   20 to 25 minutes

SPECIAL EQUIPMENT
   Cake pop sticks; small scoop

*W*hat's more irresistible than a moist, chewy macaroon? A moist, chewy macaroon smothered in dark chocolate. On a stick! These twirl-in-your-mouth pops bring a taste of the tropics indoors and easily satisfy even the strongest coconut craving. Make them for the coconut lovers in your life.

MACAROON CAKE POP BATTER

2 cups sweetened flaked coconut

½ cup sugar

3 tablespoons all-purpose flour

2 egg whites

½ teaspoon almond extract

SEMISWEET OR DARK CHOCOLATE COATING

1 cup (6 ounces) semisweet or dark chocolate chips

¼ teaspoon vegetable shortening or coconut oil

1. Preheat the oven to 350°F. Grease a baking sheet and set aside.

2. Mix together the coconut, sugar, and flour; set aside.

3. Use an electric mixer to beat the egg whites in a separate bowl until stiff. Add the egg whites and the almond extract to the coconut mixture and mix thoroughly to combine.

4. Use a small scoop to scoop portions of the batter, roll them into balls by hand, and put them on the prepared baking sheet. Bake for 20 to 25 minutes until the edges are golden. Allow to cool, then refrigerate for 30 minutes.

5. **PREPARE THE CHOCOLATE COATING:** Microwave the chocolate chips and the shortening in a microwave-safe bowl on high for 30 seconds; remove and stir. Return to the microwave if not thoroughly melted, and microwave in 15-second intervals until smooth and creamy. (Do not overheat or the chocolate will scorch).

6. Insert a cake pop stick in the center of each macaroon ball, then dip into the melted chocolate to coat. Set the finished macaroon pops in a stand, tall drinking glass, or foam block until ready to serve.

grand marnier® brownie truffles

YIELD   32 truffles

PREP   25 minutes

BAKE   25 minutes

SPECIAL EQUIPMENT
        Small scoop

Signature Brownie recipe for
8 × 8-inch pan (page 19)

2 tablespoons Grand Marnier®

1½ to 2 cups confectioners' sugar

If you've never tasted Grand Marnier®, I highly recommend it. It's an aromatic French liqueur, created in 1880, that blends premium cognac with wild tropical oranges from the Caribbean. It's that touch of orange that transforms this domestic yet bold brownie truffle into an international taste sensation. Serve with snifters of Grand Marnier®, neat, or cups of espresso.

1. Preheat the oven to 350°F. Grease an 8 × 8-inch pan and set aside.

2. Prepare the signature brownie batter according to directions. Bake in the prepared pan for 25 minutes. Allow to cool.

3. Remove the cooled brownie from the pan and trim away the crisp edges. Place the brownie in a large mixing bowl or food processor. Add the Grand Marnier® and mix thoroughly with an electric mixer or food processor until the consistency is pliable enough to form small balls. (Chill for 30 minutes if too soft.)

4. Use a small scoop to measure out a portion of the brownie mixture and form it into a ball by hand. Repeat using the remainder of the brownie mixture.

5. Chill the truffles in an airtight container in the refrigerator for at least 30 minutes. Roll the truffles in the confectioners' sugar to evenly coat just before serving.

Grand Marnier® is a registered trademark of Societé des Produits Marnier Lapostolle

brownie cake pops

YIELD 28 cake pops

PREP 20 minutes

BAKE 25 minutes

SPECIAL EQUIPMENT

Cake pop sticks; small scoop

rim. Crumble. Scoop. Roll. Freeze. Serve. Six simple steps to a completely captivating confection. With a rich cocoa core and a creamy white chocolate exterior, these sophisticated "lollipops" are quite simply bite-size balls of chocolate cheer. Oops! Almost forgot the seventh step: Enjoy!

BROWNIE CAKE POP BATTER

12 tablespoons (1½ sticks) salted butter, melted

1¾ cups sugar

2 large eggs

2 teaspoons pure vanilla extract

1¼ cups all-purpose flour

¾ cup 100% baking cocoa

½ teaspoon baking powder

¼ teaspoon salt

WHITE CHOCOLATE COATING

2 cups (12 ounces) white chocolate chips

½ teaspoon vegetable shortening or coconut oil

1. Preheat the oven to 350°F. Grease an 8 × 8-inch pan with butter or nonstick cooking spray and set aside.

2. Use an electric mixer set on lowest speed or a spatula to mix the melted butter and sugar until well combined. Add the eggs and vanilla and mix on low speed until blended. Whisk together the flour, cocoa, baking powder, and salt in a separate bowl. Add the dry ingredients to the wet ingredients gradually; mix thoroughly.

3. Spoon the batter into the prepared pan and bake for 25 minutes. Set aside to cool.

4. Remove the cooled brownie from the pan and trim away the crisp edges. Put the brownie in a large bowl or a food processor. Use an electric mixer or a food processor to mix thoroughly until pliable enough to form small balls.

5. Use a small scoop to measure out a portion of the brownie mixture and roll into a ball by hand. Repeat with the remainder of the brownie mixture. Place a cake pop stick into each ball and freeze for 30 minutes.

6. **PREPARE THE WHITE CHOCOLATE COATING:** Microwave the white chocolate chips and shortening in a microwave-safe bowl on high for 30 seconds; remove and stir. Return to microwave if not thoroughly melted, and microwave in 15-second intervals until smooth and creamy. (Do not overheat or the chocolate will scorch.)

7. Dip each chilled cake pop into the melted chocolate to coat. Place in a stand, tall drinking glass, or foam block until the coating has set. Chill in the refrigerator until ready to serve.

blonde amaretto truffles

YIELD	36 truffles
PREP	25 minutes
BAKE	25 to 27 minutes

*E*verything about these truffles is golden: butter, brown sugar, eggs, vanilla—the taste! Even the amaretto, the almond-flavored Italian liqueur at the heart of this recipe, is a lovely shade of amber. Make these for your sweetie next Valentine's Day.

1½ cups light brown sugar, packed

12 tablespoons (1½ sticks) salted butter, melted

2 large eggs

2 teaspoons pure vanilla extract

1½ cups all-purpose flour

1 teaspoon baking powder

½ teaspoon salt

2 tablespoons amaretto

1 tablespoon pure almond extract

1½ to 2 cups confectioners' sugar, for coating

1. Preheat the oven to 325°F. Grease a 9 × 13-inch pan and set aside.

2. Use an electric mixer set on the lowest speed or a spatula to combine the brown sugar with the melted butter and mix thoroughly. Add the eggs and vanilla; mix until well combined. Add the flour, baking powder, and salt and mix thoroughly. Spread the batter in the prepared pan and bake for 25 to 27 minutes (they will be slightly underdone). Allow to cool.

3. Remove the blonde brownies from the pan and trim away the crisp edges. Put the brownie in a mixing bowl or a food processor (it's okay if it breaks into pieces). Use an electric mixer or a food processor to mix thoroughly until pliable enough to form small balls. Mix in the amaretto and almond extract. Chill in the refrigerator for 30 minutes.

4. Use a small scoop to measure out a portion of the blonde brownie mixture and roll into a ball by hand. Repeat with the remainder of the blonde brownie mixture.

5. Chill the truffles in an airtight container in the refrigerator for at least 30 minutes. Just before serving, roll the truffles in the confectioners' sugar to evenly coat.

key lime truffles

YIELD   32 truffles

PREP   20 minutes

BAKE   25 minutes

SPECIAL EQUIPMENT
   Small scoop

B limey! These limey truffles would excite even the most reserved Brit. They're buttery and bursting with the tang of Key lime. The zest peeks through, adding a hint of green, and the fine white chocolate drizzle lends an air of elegance. Cool and refreshing, these plump confections belong on the top tier of an afternoon tea stand.

KEY LIME TRUFFLE BATTER

1½ cups sugar

12 tablespoons (1½ sticks) salted butter, melted

2 large eggs

2 teaspoons pure vanilla extract

1 tablespoon Key lime zest

2 tablespoons Key lime juice

1½ cups all-purpose flour

1 teaspoon baking powder

½ teaspoon salt

½ cup (3 ounces) white chocolate chips, chopped

WHITE CHOCOLATE DRIZZLE

½ cup (3 ounces) white chocolate chips

¼ teaspoon vegetable shortening or coconut oil

1. Preheat the oven to 325°F. Grease a 9 × 13-inch pan and set aside.

2. **PREPARE THE KEY LIME TRUFFLE BATTER:** Use an electric mixer set on the lowest speed or a spatula to combine the sugar and melted butter and mix thoroughly. Mix in the eggs and vanilla until well combined, then mix in the lime zest and juice. Add the flour, baking powder, and salt and mix thoroughly. Mix in the chopped white chocolate chips until evenly distributed.

3. Spread the batter in the prepared pan and bake for 25 minutes. Allow to cool.

4. Remove the Key lime brownies from the pan and trim away the crisp edges. Put the brownie in a large bowl or a food processor and mix until pliable enough to form small balls (refrigerate if too soft).

5. Line a baking sheet with foil or parchment paper. Use a small scoop to measure out a portion of the Key lime brownie mixture, roll it into a ball by hand, and set it on the prepared baking sheet. Repeat with the remainder of the brownie mixture. Chill in the refrigerator for 30 minutes.

6. **PREPARE THE WHITE CHOCOLATE DRIZZLE:** Microwave the white chocolate chips and shortening in a microwave-safe bowl for 30 seconds; remove and stir. Return to the microwave if not thoroughly melted, and microwave in 15-second intervals until smooth and creamy. (Do not overheat or the chocolate will scorch.)

7. Drizzle the truffles with the white chocolate and allow it to set. Transfer the truffles to an airtight container and store in the refrigerator or in a cool, dry place until ready to serve.

salted butterscotch truffles

YIELD 26 truffles

PREP 30 minutes

SPECIAL EQUIPMENT

Small scoop

BUTTERSCOTCH TRUFFLE BATTER

1 cup (6 ounces) butterscotch chips

1 tablespoon salted butter

½ cup (4 ounces) cream cheese, at room temperature

1 cup confectioners' sugar

1 teaspoon pure vanilla extract

SEMISWEET CHOCOLATE COATING

1 cup (6 ounces) semisweet chocolate chips

¼ teaspoon vegetable shortening or coconut oil

Coarse sea salt, for sprinkling

The name "butterscotch" is deceiving. It's true the candy's tawny yellow color reminds you of butter and there is butter in it, but trust me there isn't any Scotch! The word, which originated in England, is most likely derived from "scorch." That's because during the cooking process, the sugar is heated at very high temperatures. Lucky for us, we don't have to worry about scorching sugar. We can just pick up a bag of butterscotch chips at the supermarket. What tips the dessert-o-meter in favor of these creamy, smooth, buttery truffles is extraordinarily simple: A pinch of sea salt.

1. **PREPARE THE BUTTERSCOTCH TRUFFLE BATTER:** Microwave the butterscotch chips and butter in a microwave-safe bowl on high for 30 seconds; remove and stir. Return to the microwave if not thoroughly melted, and microwave in 15-second intervals until smooth. (Do not overheat or the butterscotch will scorch.)

2. Add the cream cheese to the melted butterscotch mixture and mix with a spatula until thoroughly blended. Add the confectioners' sugar and vanilla, and continue mixing until smooth and creamy. Chill in the refrigerator for 1 hour.

3. **PREPARE THE CHOCOLATE COATING:** Microwave the chocolate chips and shortening in a microwave-safe bowl on high for 30 seconds; remove and stir. Return to the microwave if not thoroughly melted, and microwave in 15-second intervals until smooth and creamy. (Do not overheat or the chocolate will scorch.)

4. Line a baking sheet with foil or parchment paper. Use a small scoop to measure out a portion of the butterscotch batter, roll it into a ball with your hands, and place it on the prepared baking sheet.

5. Dip each truffle in the chocolate coating, return to the prepared baking sheet, and sprinkle with sea salt. Allow the chocolate to set before serving.

> Chocolate dipping tools—special two- or three-tined forks, swirls, and baskets—make dipping and enrobing desserts in chocolate so much easier. Find them online or at restaurant and kitchen supply stores.

cappuccino bonbons

YIELD 32 bonbons

PREP 25 minutes

BAKE 25 minutes

SPECIAL EQUIPMENT
Small scoop

CAPPUCCINO BROWNIE BATTER

2 cups (12 ounces) semisweet chocolate chips

6 tablespoons salted butter

1 tablespoon instant espresso powder

2 teaspoons hot water

½ cup sugar

2 large eggs

1 teaspoon pure vanilla extract

¾ cup all-purpose flour

½ teaspoon baking powder

¼ teaspoon salt

1 tablespoon 100% baking cocoa

MILK CHOCOLATE GLAZE

2 cups (12 ounces) milk chocolate chips

¼ teaspoon vegetable shortening or coconut oil, plus more if needed

Coffee and chocolate are so compatible they must be related. Think about it. Both start out as beans, both are dark in color and rich in flavor. They actually share a health benefit or two and both contain caffeine. If you're a coffee aficionado, chocoholic, or both, you'll appreciate the triple jolt of choco-coffee in these little bites.

1. Preheat the oven to 350°F. Grease an 8 × 8-inch pan and set aside.

2. PREPARE THE CAPPUCCINO BROWNIE BATTER: Microwave the chocolate chips and butter in a microwave-safe bowl on high for 30 seconds; remove and stir. Return to the microwave if not thoroughly melted, and microwave in 15-second intervals until smooth and creamy. (Do not overheat or the chocolate will scorch.)

3. Mix the espresso powder with the hot water until dissolved. Mix together the sugar and eggs until well combined in a separate bowl. Stir the espresso mixture and the vanilla into the egg mixture. Fold the egg mixture into the melted chocolate and butter and mix thoroughly. Add the flour, baking powder, salt and cocoa and mix thoroughly.

4. Pour the batter into the prepared pan and bake for 25 minutes. Allow to cool.

5. Remove the cooled brownie from the pan and trim away the crisp edges. Put the brownie in a large mixing bowl or a food processor (it's okay if it breaks into pieces). Use an electric mixer or a food processor to mix thoroughly until the consistency is pliable enough to form small balls. Use a small scoop to measure a portion of the cappuccino brownie mixture and roll it into a small ball by hand. Repeat with the remainder of the brownie mixture. Chill the bonbons in the freezer for 30 minutes.

6. PREPARE THE MILK CHOCOLATE GLAZE: Microwave the chocolate chips and shortening in a microwave-safe bowl on high for 30 seconds; remove and stir. Return to the microwave if not thoroughly melted, and microwave in 15-second intervals until smooth and creamy. Stir in another ¼ teaspoon shortening if the glaze is too thick. (Do not overheat or the chocolate will scorch.)

7. Line a baking sheet with foil or parchment paper. Dip the bonbons into the chocolate glaze and place on the prepared baking sheet until the glaze has set. Chill in the refrigerator until ready to serve.

glazed brownie bonbons

YIELD	32 bonbons
PREP	20 minutes
BAKE	10 minutes per batch
SPECIAL EQUIPMENT	Small scoop; pan with orb-shaped recesses

BROWNIE BONBONS

2 cups (12 ounces) semisweet chocolate chips

6 tablespoons unsalted butter

2 large eggs

1 teaspoon pure vanilla extract

½ cup granulated sugar

¾ cup all-purpose flour

½ teaspoon baking powder

¼ teaspoon salt

1 tablespoon 100% baking cocoa

VANILLA GLAZE

1½ cups confectioners' sugar

3 to 4 tablespoons milk

1 teaspoon pure vanilla extract

*D*id you ever hear someone say: "I don't spend my days lounging on the couch eating bonbons"? The implication is that only those with time on their hands can enjoy such a rich indulgence. Well, this recipe dispels that myth. First, my Glazed Brownie Bonbons are simple to make. Second, the ingredients are staples in every baker's pantry. Third, you can whip up a batch in half an hour.

So what exactly is a bonbon? The term comes from a childlike repetition of "bon," the French word for "good," and refers to a confection coated in chocolate with fruit or nuts in the center. My bonbons have a brownie core coated with a sugar and vanilla glaze, which may cause kids and adults alike to rename them "yum-yums."

1. Preheat the oven to 350°F. Grease a pan with orb-shaped recesses (each section resembles a half globe) and set aside.

2. **PREPARE THE BROWNIE BONBONS:** Microwave the chocolate chips and butter in microwave-safe bowl on high for 30 seconds; remove and stir. Return to the microwave if not thoroughly melted, and microwave in 15-second intervals until smooth and creamy. (Do not overheat or the chocolate will scorch.)

3. Mix together the eggs, vanilla, and sugar in a separate bowl. Stir the egg mixture into the melted chocolate mixture. Add the flour, baking powder, salt, and cocoa, and mix thoroughly.

4. Use a small scoop to measure a portion of the batter into each orb-shaped recess of the pan. Bake for 10 minutes, until centers rise and fall and edges begin to crisp. Prepare additional bonbons using the remainder of the bonbon batter, if necessary. Allow to cool.

5. **PREPARE THE VANILLA GLAZE:** Mix together the confectioners' sugar, milk, and vanilla until smooth and creamy.

6. Drizzle the glaze over the bonbons and allow to set for 10 to 15 minutes before serving.

chocolate-cherry brownie bonbons

YIELD   32 bonbons

PREP   25 minutes

BAKE   25 minutes

SPECIAL EQUIPMENT
   Small scoop

Is there a better marriage of flavors than cherry and chocolate? Nope! And this recipe brings these soul mates together in a bitter-and-sweet fusion of semisweet and dark chocolate plus maraschino cherries. Fall in love with dessert all over again.

BROWNIE BATTER

2 cups (12 ounces) semisweet chocolate chips

6 tablespoons salted butter, softened

2 large eggs

1 teaspoon pure vanilla extract

½ cup sugar

¾ cup all-purpose flour

½ teaspoon baking powder

¼ teaspoon salt

1 tablespoon 100% baking cocoa

1 (10-ounce) jar maraschino cherries

DARK CHOCOLATE DIP

2 cups (12 ounces) dark chocolate chips

¼ to ½ teaspoon vegetable shortening or coconut oil

1. Preheat the oven to 350°F. Grease an 8 × 8-inch pan and set aside.

2. PREPARE THE BROWNIE BATTER: Microwave the chocolate chips and butter in microwave-safe bowl on high for 30 seconds; remove and stir. Return to the microwave if not thoroughly melted, and microwave in 15-second intervals until smooth and creamy.

3. Use an electric mixer set on the lowest speed or a spatula to mix together eggs, vanilla, and sugar in a separate bowl. Blend egg mixture into the melted chocolate mixture. Add flour, baking powder, salt, and cocoa and mix well by hand or using lowest setting on mixer. Pour batter into the prepared pan and bake for 25 minutes, until slightly underbaked. Set aside to cool.

4. Drain the cherries, reserving 2 tablespoons of the liquid. Cut cherries into quarters and set aside.

5. Remove the cooled brownie from pan and trim away the crisp edges. Put the brownie in a large a mixing bowl (it's okay if it breaks into pieces) and add 1 tablespoon of cherry juice. Mix thoroughly using an electric mixer until the consistency is pliable enough to form small balls. Mix in remaining tablespoon of cherry juice, if needed.

6. Fill half of a small scoop with brownie mixture. Place a piece of cherry in the center, and then fill the remainder of the scoop with the brownie mixture. Form into a small ball by hand, and repeat with rest of the brownie mixture and cherries. Freeze the bonbons for 30 minutes.

7. PREPARE THE CHOCOLATE FOR DIPPING: Melt chocolate chips and ¼ teaspoon of the shortening as per step 2. Stir in another ¼ teaspoon of shortening if the chocolate mixture is too thick.

8. Line a baking sheet with foil or parchment paper. Dip chilled bonbons in the melted chocolate mixture and place them on the prepared baking sheet until chocolate sets. Store in the refrigerator until ready to serve.

brownie bites

Expect the unexpected from these bite-size treats. Some surprise you with jelly centers, others with marshmallows, graham cracker crumbs, or pretzels. Most of the recipes here yield at least twenty-four bites, so you can please a lot of people all at once.

crème brûlée brownie bites

YIELD   28 brownie bites

PREP   25 minutes

BAKE   12 minutes per batch

SPECIAL EQUIPMENT

Mini muffin pan; culinary torch

Signature Brownie recipe for
8 × 8-inch pan (page 19)

1 package (3.4 ounces) instant
vanilla pudding

2 cups milk

1 cup sugar

Crème brûlée is one of my favorite desserts. Cracking through the caramelized sugar to the creamy custard underneath is one of life's simple pleasures. How could I improve on perfection? Once again my imagination turned to chocolate. I could bake bite-size brownies in a mini muffin pan, and once they'd cooled, top them with a layer of pudding and burnt sugar. That would give me a rich chocolate bottom, velvety custard middle, and sweet crunchy crown. In other words, a sure-fire winner!

If you don't have a culinary torch for caramelizing sugar, put your brownie bites under the broiler of a gas oven, or simply heat a metal spoon over a flame and press it into the sugar.

1. Preheat the oven to 350°F. Grease a mini muffin pan with nonstick cooking spray and set aside.

2. Prepare the signature brownie batter according to instructions. Fill each muffin cup two-thirds full with the batter. Bake for 12 minutes, until muffins rise in center, then fall, and edges begin to crisp. Allow to cool before removing the bites from the pan.

3. Pour the pudding mix into a bowl and mix in the milk, beating for 2 minutes or as directed on the package. Allow the pudding to set, about 5 minutes. Spoon some pudding on top of each brownie bite, then sprinkle the tops with a generous, even layer of the sugar.

4. Set a culinary torch on high. Pass the flame over the sugar slowly to scorch the surface. (Or use one of the alternate methods described above to caramelize the sugar.)

cannoli brownie bites

YIELD 28 bites

PREP 20 minutes

BAKE 12 minutes

SPECIAL EQUIPMENT
Mini muffin pan; pastry bag and tip, optional

Signature Brownie recipe for
8 × 8-inch pan (page 19)

CANNOLI FILLING

¾ cup (6 ounces) cream cheese, at room temperature

4 tablespoons (½ stick) salted butter, at room temperature

⅓ cup ricotta cheese

1 teaspoon pure vanilla extract

2 cups confectioners' sugar

½ cup mini semisweet chocolate chips

Once again, I took a popular dessert (in this case an Italian pastry called a cannoli, which means "little tube"), simplified the recipe, and found a way to sneak in a little chocolate. For traditional cannolis, you have to make shells, or tubes, out of dough, fry one or two at a time, and then carefully stuff them with filling. This recipe cuts the prep time in half by using bite-size brownies to hold the sweet and creamy cheese filling. The end result is every bit as rich and satisfying as its Italian cousin—and so much easier to prepare and eat.

1. Preheat the oven to 350°F. Grease a mini muffin pan with nonstick cooking spray and set aside.

2. Prepare the signature brownie batter according to directions. Fill each muffin cup two-thirds full with the batter. Bake for 12 minutes, until center rises and falls and edges begin to crisp. Remove the pan from the oven and indent the center of each brownie bite with a small round object, such as a soda bottle top. When the pan is warm to the touch, turn the mini bites gently to make sure they are not sticking to the sides. When cool, remove the mini bites by hand, or turn the pan over to release them.

3. **PREPARE THE CANNOLI FILLING:** Mix together the cream cheese, butter, ricotta, and vanilla until smooth and creamy. Add the confectioners' sugar gradually, and mix until well blended.

4. Scoop 1 tablespoon of the cannoli filling onto the indentation in each cooled brownie. Use a pastry bag to pipe the filling, if you'd like. Sprinkle with the mini chocolate chips, and chill until ready to serve.

cookie dough brownie bites

YIELD 28 pieces

PREP 20 minutes

BAKE 12 minutes

SPECIAL EQUIPMENT

Mini muffin pan; small scoop

Signature Brownie recipe for
8 × 8-inch pan (page 19)

RAW COOKIE DOUGH FILLING

12 tablespoons (1½ sticks) salted
butter, at room temperature

¾ cup light brown sugar, packed

⅓ cup granulated sugar

1½ teaspoons pure vanilla extract

1½ cups all-purpose flour

2 tablespoons milk

SEMISWEET CHOCOLATE DRIZZLE

1 cup semisweet chocolate chips

¼ teaspoon vegetable shortening
or coconut oil

Here's a riddle: What do you call a dollop of cookie dough hugged by fudgy brownie batter? Answer: Every mother's dream dessert. That's because this single-serving treat fits nicely in a lunchbox and features two kid favorites—chocolate and buttery, brown sugary cookie dough. Since this recipe makes 28 brownie bites, there are plenty to spare. Why not pack two so your child can share?

1. Preheat the oven to 350°F. Grease a mini muffin pan with nonstick cooking spray and set aside.

2. Prepare the signature brownie recipe according to directions. Fill each muffin cup two-thirds full with the batter. Bake for 12 minutes, until muffins rise in the center, then fall, and edges begin to crisp. Remove the pan from the oven and indent the center of each brownie bite with a small round object, such as a soda bottle top. When the pan is warm to the touch, turn the mini bites gently to make sure they are not sticking to the sides. When cool, remove the mini bites by hand, or turn the pan over to release them.

3. **PREPARE THE RAW COOKIE DOUGH FILLING:** Mix the butter, brown sugar, white sugar, vanilla, flour, and milk until smooth and creamy. Use a small scoop to measure portions of the cookie dough and place them on the indentation in the center of each cooled brownie bite.

4. **PREPARE THE SEMISWEET CHOCOLATE DRIZZLE:** Microwave the chocolate chips and shortening in a microwave-safe bowl on high for 30 seconds; remove and stir. Return to the microwave if not thoroughly melted, and microwave in 15-second intervals until smooth and creamy. (Do not overheat or the chocolate will scorch.)

5. Drizzle the chocolate topping over the top of each brownie bite.

peppermint pattie brownie bites

C *hocolate topped with a peppermint pattie, crowned with melted semisweet chocolate. Is that a chocolate lover's dream come true? It's like having a mini celebration in your mouth. Try one, or two, or three. Your sweet tooth will thank you.*

Signature Brownie recipe for 8 × 8-inch pan (page 19)

PEPPERMINT PATTIE FILLING

4 cups confectioners' sugar

½ cup corn syrup

3 tablespoons vegetable shortening or coconut oil

2 teaspoons pure peppermint extract

CHOCOLATE TOPPING

1 cup (6 ounces) semisweet chocolate chips

¼ teaspoon vegetable shortening or coconut oil

1. Preheat the oven to 350°F. Grease a mini muffin pan with nonstick cooking spray and set aside.

2. Prepare the signature brownie batter according to directions. Fill each muffin cup two-thirds full with the batter. Bake for 12 minutes, until muffins rise in the center, then fall, and edges begin to crisp. Allow to cool before removing the brownie bites from the pan.

3. **MAKE THE PEPPERMINT PATTIE FILLING:** Combine the confectioners' sugar, corn syrup, shortening, and peppermint extract. Use an electric mixer set on the lowest speed or a spatula to beat until firm enough to roll into a ball.

4. Place the ball of peppermint dough between two pieces of parchment paper and, using a rolling pin, roll out the dough until ¼-inch thick overall. Use a 1-inch round cookie cutter to cut out 28 patties. Place each peppermint pattie on top of a cooled brownie bite.

5. **PREPARE THE CHOCOLATE TOPPING:** Microwave the chocolate chips and shortening in a microwave-safe bowl on high for 30 seconds; remove and stir. Return to the microwave if not thoroughly melted, and microwave in 15-second intervals until smooth and creamy. (Do not overheat or the chocolate will scorch.)

6. Pour 1 tablespoon of the melted chocolate topping over each peppermint pattie; allow to set. Serve when the chocolate topping is firm.

s'mores brownie bites

YIELD 28 bites

PREP 20 minutes

BAKE 12 minutes

SPECIAL EQUIPMENT
Mini muffin pan

Signature Brownie recipe for
8 × 8-inch pan (page 19)

S'MORES FILLING

1½ cups graham cracker crumbs

6 tablespoons salted butter, melted

1½ to 2 cups marshmallow fluff

½ cup mini semisweet
chocolate chips

According to Hershey's website, the first printed s'mores recipe appeared in the Girl Scout Handbook in 1927. Folklore tells us this campfire treat was so named because everyone who tasted one asked for "some more." The original recipe called for a Hershey's milk chocolate bar, graham crackers, and marshmallows. Not being the outdoorsy type, I came up with this indoor version to surprise my granddaughters. It starts with my Signature Brownie recipe (as so many of my creations do), includes buttery graham cracker crumbs and a fluff of warm marshmallow at its center, and ends with chocolate chips.

When I explained to my granddaughters how people roast marshmallows over campfires then sandwich them, along with a candy bar, between two graham crackers, they giggled and said, "That sure sounds messy and like a lot of trouble. We'll just have s'more of your brownie bites, Grandma."

1. Preheat the oven to 350°F. Grease a mini muffin pan with nonstick cooking spray and set aside.

2. Prepare the signature brownie batter according to directions. Fill each muffin cup two-thirds full with the batter. Bake for 12 minutes, until muffins rise in the center, then fall, and edges begin to crisp. Remove the pan from the oven and indent the center of each brownie bite with a small round object, such as a soda bottle top. When the pan is warm to the touch, turn the mini bites gently to make sure they are not sticking to the sides. When cool, remove the mini bites by hand, or turn the pan over to release them.

3. **PREPARE THE S'MORES FILLING:** Mix together the graham cracker crumbs and melted butter until thoroughly combined. Scoop about 2 tablespoons of the s'mores filling into the indentation in each cooled brownie bite.

4. Microwave the marshmallow fluff in a microwave-safe bowl on high for 10 to 15 seconds, and then spoon it over the brownie bites.

5. Sprinkle the tops of the brownie bites with the mini chocolate chips and serve.

pbj and graham cracker bites

YIELD 14 bites

PREP 15 minutes, plus 1 hour
in the freezer

SPECIAL EQUIPMENT
Small scoop

1 cup creamy peanut butter
(all-natural recommended)

½ cup light brown sugar, packed

1 cup graham cracker crumbs

½ cup strawberry jelly

2 cups (12 ounces) milk
chocolate chips

½ teaspoon vegetable shortening
or coconut oil

A better name for these treats might be: PBJ Surprise! That's because kids (and grown-ups, too) don't expect the squirt of strawberry jelly when they bite into them for the first time. The graham cracker crumbs add a little crunch and the melted chocolate is a fuss-free way to top the whole thing off. These peanut buttery bites deliver a taste and texture combination that elicits smiles all around.

1. Line a baking sheet with parchment paper. Mix together the peanut butter, brown sugar, and graham cracker crumbs. Fill half of a small scoop with batter, add ¼ to ½ teaspoon strawberry jelly, then fill the rest of the scoop with batter. Roll into a ball using your hands and place on the prepared baking sheet. Repeat with the remaining batter and jelly. Chill in the freezer for 1 hour.

2. Microwave the chocolate chips and shortening in a microwave-safe bowl on high for 30 seconds; remove and stir. Return to the microwave if not completely melted, and microwave for 15-second intervals until melted and smooth. (Do not overheat or the chocolate will scorch.)

3. Remove the PBJ bites from the freezer, dip each one into the melted chocolate, and return to the parchment paper until the chocolate is set. Store in the refrigerator until ready to serve.

cookies and cream fudge bites

YIELD   32 to 36 squares

PREP   12 to 15 minutes

CHILL   45 minutes to 1 hour

1 (14-ounce) can sweetened condensed milk

3 cups (18 ounces) white chocolate chips

4 cups BROWNIE BRITTLE™ (one 5-ounce bag = 1 cup chopped) or chocolate wafers chopped into small pieces

ere's one recipe you won't even break a sweat over. No baking. Four ingredients. Four prep steps that take no more than 12 minutes. The rest is chill time. But the end result is so delicious you can probably convince family and friends you spent the better part of the afternoon in the kitchen.

1. Grease a 9 × 13-inch pan with nonstick cooking spray and set aside.

2. Microwave the sweetened condensed milk and white chocolate chips in a microwave-safe bowl on high for 30 seconds; remove and stir. Return to the microwave if not thoroughly melted, and microwave in 15-second intervals until smooth and creamy. (Do not overheat or the chocolate will scorch.)

3. Stir the chopped BROWNIE BRITTLE™ into the melted chocolate mixture and pour into the prepared pan. Chill until set, 45 minutes to 1 hour.

4. Cut into small squares and enjoy!

dulce de leche mini muffins

YIELD   38 mini muffins

PREP   20 minutes

BAKE   18 to 20 minutes

SPECIAL EQUIPMENT
       Mini muffin pan; medium scoop;
       pastry bag with tips

Blonde Brownie recipe (page 20)

Half of a 13-ounce can of dulce de leche (use remainder to make frosting, below)

DULCE DE LECHE FROSTING
Half of a 13-ounce can of dulce de leche

1 (8-ounce) package cream cheese, softened

1 teaspoon pure vanilla extract

*D*ulce *means sweet and* leche *means milk in Spanish. And it is this "sweet milk" that gives these mini morsels such a big boost up the sweetness meter. Pairing dulce de leche with my Blonde Brownie recipe results in creamy, caramel-y, bite-size pieces of heaven. Pop one in your mouth and see if you don't agree. The dulce de leche frosting makes these bites doubly good, but if you prefer, you can dust them with confectioners' sugar instead.*

By the way, you can usually find cans of dulce de leche in the baking aisle alongside evaporated and condensed milk.

1. Preheat the oven to 325°F. Spray a mini muffin pan with nonstick cooking spray and set aside.

2. Prepare the blonde brownie batter and set aside.

3. Scoop the dulce de leche into a microwave-safe dish. Microwave on high for 30 seconds; remove and stir. Slowly pour the dulce de leche into the blondie batter, using a butter knife to gently swirl it into the batter; be careful not to overmix.

4. Use a medium scoop to fill each cup of the muffin pan about two-thirds full. Bake for 18 to 20 minutes, until they start to turn golden. Cool completely, and then remove the mini muffins from the pan. Repeat with the remaining batter.

5. MAKE THE DULCE DE LECHE FROSTING: Use an electric mixer to mix together the dulce de leche, cream cheese, and vanilla until soft and creamy.

6. Fill a pastry bag with the frosting and decorate the top of each cooled mini muffin.

> To prevent mini muffins, bars, and madeleines from sticking, spray the pan with nonstick cooking spray or line with paper baking cups.

brownies à la mode

YIELD	8 servings
PREP	10 minutes
BAKE	25 minutes

Signature Brownie recipe for 8 × 8-inch pan (page 19)

Ice cream flavor of your choice

1 (12-ounce) jar of fudge or other favorite sundae topping

I think of these as brownies à la "moderne." Instead of plopping a scoop of ice cream on a square brownie, I changed the shape (to make it more muffin-like) and created a pocket for the ice cream. It's pretty compact, and the ice cream melts into (and not off) the brownie. Of course, smothering it with hot fudge is a holdover from the good old days.

1. Preheat the oven to 350°F. Grease a standard muffin pan with butter or nonstick spray and set aside.

2. Prepare the signature brownie batter according to directions. Fill each muffin cup two-thirds full with the batter. Bake for 25 minutes, until center rises and falls and edges begin to crisp. Set the brownies aside until the pan is warm to the touch.

3. Use the bottom of a glass to press down on the center of each brownie to create a bowl-shaped indentation. Let the brownies cool completely before removing them from the pan.

4. Add a scoop of ice cream to the indentation in each brownie. Serve topped with hot fudge or topping of your choice.

cookie dough ice cream sandwiches

YIELD   5 or 6 servings

PREP   20 to 25 minutes plus 1 hour in the freezer

12 tablespoons (1½ sticks) salted butter, melted

¾ cup light brown sugar, packed

⅓ cup granulated sugar

1½ teaspoons pure vanilla extract

1½ cups all-purpose flour

¾ cup mini semisweet chocolate chips

2 tablespoons milk

1 quart vanilla ice cream (or flavor of your choice)

The cookie dough fans in my house adore these. That's because they're a happy departure from the black-and-white ice cream sandwiches found in supermarket freezers. The ingredient that really makes this recipe a winner is butter so be sure to use 100 percent sweet cream salted butter. It makes all the difference. And while vanilla is still the number 1 flavor of ice cream in the world (and an excellent companion to cookie dough), you might want to try something more adventurous, like cherry or mint chocolate chip.

1. Use an electric mixer to blend together the melted butter, brown and granulated sugars, and vanilla extract. Add the flour and mix thoroughly. Use a spatula or large spoon to mix in the chocolate chips and just enough of the milk to allow the batter to be easily spread into a pan.

2. Press the batter firmly and evenly into a 9 × 13-inch pan. Cover the pan with foil and put it in the freezer for 1 hour.

3. Allow the ice cream to soften slightly before removing the cookie dough from the freezer. Use a round or, preferably, square cookie cutter to cut out 10 to 12 frozen cookies and place them on a sheet of parchment paper. Spread the softened ice cream evenly over half of the frozen cookies and place the remaining cookies on top to form sandwiches. Scrape the excess ice cream from the sides. Place the cookie dough sandwiches in a covered container and return them to the freezer until firm before serving.

brownie ice cream sandwiches

YIELD 5 servings

PREP 25 minutes

BAKE 11 minutes

SPECIAL EQUIPMENT
Large scoop

2 cups (12 ounces) semisweet chocolate chips

6 tablespoons salted butter

2 large eggs

1 teaspoon pure vanilla extract

½ cup sugar

1 cup all-purpose flour

½ teaspoon baking powder

¼ teaspoon salt

1 tablespoon 100% baking cocoa

Ice cream flavor(s) of your choice

hese ice cream sandwiches can't help but be the center of attention—especially at a kid's birthday party—and they're so much more fun than a frosted sheet cake. Choose several different ice cream flavors (think colorful) and let your guests pick their favorites. One of the advantages of this dessert is it can be whipped up in advance. But don't feel like you have to throw a party to serve these. Make them any time and stash them in your freezer for those nights when there's simply no time to bake.

1. Preheat the oven to 350°F. Grease a baking sheet and set aside.

2. Microwave the chocolate chips and butter in a microwave-safe bowl on high for 30 seconds; remove and stir. Return to the microwave if not completely melted, and microwave in 15-second intervals until smooth and creamy. (Do not overheat or the chocolate will scorch.)

3. Use an electric mixer or a spatula to mix together the eggs, vanilla, and sugar in a separate bowl. Blend the egg mixture into the melted chocolate mixture. Add the flour, baking powder, salt, and cocoa and mix on low speed until thoroughly combined.

4. Use large scoop to measure 10 portions of the batter and drop them onto the prepared baking sheet. Bake for 11 minutes, until edges begin to crisp. Allow to cool completely.

5. Place a scoop of ice cream in the center of one brownie, then place another brownie on top to form a sandwich. Trim off excess ice cream from the sides. Repeat with the remaining brownies.

6. Wrap each ice cream sandwich individually in plastic wrap and store in the freezer for 2 to 3 months.

ice cream tart with brownie brittle crust

YIELD 16 servings

PREP 20 minutes

BAKE 8 minutes

SPECIAL EQUIPMENT
11-inch tart pan

*E*nd your dinner on a high note. Not only is this tart eye-catching, it's full of surprises. The crust is crunchy. The chocolate shell on top has a snap to it. The ice cream holds its own in the middle until it melts in your mouth. And depending on the garnish you opt for, you can add one last sweet, salty, or nutty burst of flavor. Whichever you choose, your guests will be singing your praises.

2½ cups BROWNIE BRITTLE™ (one 5-ounce bag = 1 cup crushed) or chocolate wafers crushed in a food processor

10 tablespoons (1 stick plus 2 tablespoons) salted butter, melted

3 cups vanilla ice cream or flavor of your choice

1½ cups (9 ounces) dark chocolate chips

¼ cup vegetable shortening or coconut oil

Whipped cream, sea salt, chopped nuts, toffee bits, or sprinkles, for garnish

1. Preheat the oven to 350°F. Spray an 11-inch tart pan with nonstick cooking spray and set aside.

2. Mix together the BROWNIE BRITTLE™ and melted butter. Press the crumb mixture into the bottom and up the sides of prepared tart pan. Bake for 8 minutes, and then set aside to cool.

3. Put the ice cream in a medium-size bowl and allow to soften slightly. Blend ice cream using an electric mixer until it is soft enough to spread. Spread the ice cream evenly over the brownie crust, and return the pan to the freezer so the ice cream freezes again.

4. Microwave the chocolate chips and shortening in a microwave-safe bowl on high for 30 seconds; remove and stir. Return to microwave if not completely melted, and microwave in 15-second intervals until smooth and creamy. (Do not overheat or the chocolate will scorch.) Allow to cool.

5. Remove the ice cream tart from the freezer and pour the chocolate topping over the ice cream, creating a hard shell. Garnish with your choice of whipped cream, sea salt, chopped nuts, toffee bits, or sprinkles.

rich chocolate banana and brownie shake

YIELD	1 serving
PREP	5 minutes

3 scoops chocolate ice cream

1 large banana, peeled and frozen

¼ cup Brownie Filling (recipe, page 43)

Had a rough day at the office? Dog chew up your sneakers? Can't find the perfect outfit for your in-laws' anniversary party? On the outs with your neighbor? Take a deep breath and toss a banana in the freezer. This shake provides a sweet solution to life's many challenges, and has all the necessary ingredients to lift your spirits and alter your perspective. (Take one to your neighbor as a peace offering.)

Mix all the ingredients in a blender until smooth and creamy. Pour into a glass and enjoy!

brownie waffle cones

YIELD 12 servings

PREP 12 minutes

BAKE 2 minutes per cone

SPECIAL EQUIPMENT

Waffle cone maker with cone-shaped form and utensil; medium scoop

2 cups (12 ounces) semisweet chocolate chips

6 tablespoons salted butter

4 large eggs

1 teaspoon pure vanilla extract

½ cup sugar

¾ cup all-purpose flour

½ teaspoon baking powder

¼ teaspoon salt

1 tablespoon 100% baking cocoa

Ice cream flavor(s) of choice

What's more fun than an ice cream-filled waffle cone from the food court at your favorite mall? How about a brownie-flavored waffle cone made fresh in your own kitchen? The aroma alone is worth the effort. Serve them at your child's next birthday party. No plates, no forks—just plenty of ice cream grins.

1. Preheat the waffle cone maker to medium heat.

2. Microwave the chocolate chips and butter in a microwave-safe bowl on high for 30 seconds; remove and stir. Return to the microwave if not thoroughly melted, and microwave in 15-second intervals until smooth and creamy. (Do not overheat or the chocolate will scorch.)

3. Use an electric mixer set on the lowest speed or a spatula to mix together the eggs, sugar, and vanilla. Add the egg mixture to the melted chocolate mixture and stir until smooth. Add the flour, baking powder, salt, and cocoa and mix until fully blended.

4. Use a medium scoop to measure out a portion of the batter and pour it onto the center of the waffle maker. Close the lid and cook for 2 minutes. Open the lid and allow the waffle to cool slightly before lifting it off the heat with a spatula. Use a cone-shaped utensil to wrap the warm waffle around the ice cream cone form, then set aside to cool. Repeat with the remaining batter to create 12 waffle cones.

5. Fill the brownie waffle cones with scoops of ice cream and serve. Alternatively, waffle cones can be made ahead and stored in an airtight container for future use.

brownie mudslide cocktail

YIELD   1 cocktail

PREP   5 minutes

1 ounce rum

1 ounce Kahlúa® or other
coffee-flavored liqueur

1 ounce Baileys® Irish Cream
(Irish whiskey and cream liqueur)

1 tablespoon Brownie Filling
(recipe, page 43)

1 ounce half-and-half

Whipped cream, for topping

Pinch of cocoa powder or ground
cinnamon, for garnish, optional

A welcome break from ho-hum wine and beer, this fudgy mudslide is like indulging in a drink and dessert at the same time. Most mudslide recipes call for vodka, but I prefer rum, for the simple reason that rum adds another layer of flavor that blends so perfectly with the tastes of coffee and cream. Dusting the whipped cream with a pinch of cocoa or cinnamon spices up this spirited drink even more.

1. Combine the rum, Kahlúa®, Baileys®, brownie filling, and half-and-half in a mixer and blend until smooth.

2. Pour into a cocktail shaker with ½ cup ice. Shake to chill, and then pour into a glass.

Kahlúa® is a registered trademark of The Absolut Company Aktiebolag
Baileys® is a registered trademark of R & A Bailey and Co.

fancy brownie desserts

When a meal warrants a grand finale, each of the recipes in this chapter rises to the occasion. They're a treat for the senses: aromatic, lovely to look at, and an intoxicating blend of the finest flavors and ingredients. To create a lasting impression, make one of these. Then, take a bow.

vanilla-bean brownie pound cake

YIELD   12 servings

PREP   25 minutes

BAKE   55 minutes

SPECIAL EQUIPMENT

Offset spatula

BROWNIE LAYER

2 cups (12 ounces) semisweet chocolate chips

6 tablespoons salted butter

2 large eggs

1 teaspoon pure vanilla extract

½ cup sugar

½ cup all-purpose flour

½ teaspoon baking powder

¼ teaspoon salt

1 tablespoon 100% baking cocoa

VANILLA-BEAN CAKE LAYER

1 cup all-purpose flour

½ teaspoon baking powder

¼ teaspoon baking soda

¼ teaspoon salt

⅔ cup sugar

1 vanilla bean, seeds scraped (or substitute 2 teaspoons pure vanilla extract)

4 tablespoons (½ stick) unsalted butter, softened

1 large egg, at room temperature

⅔ cup low-fat buttermilk, at room temperature

Here's a new take on that timeless dessert—pound cake. Only my version has a brownie layer underneath the vanilla-bean layer. This two-toned cake is super moist and makes an attractive, tasty foundation for ice cream, whipped cream, fruit—or all of the above. And don't be afraid to use a real vanilla bean (just make sure it's not dried out). Simply split the pod lengthwise with a small, pointed knife and scrape the seeds (they're more like tiny black specks) into the bowl. That's all there is to it. While vanilla beans are a bit pricey, you'll be amazed at how much more vibrant and vanilla-y the flavor is.

1. Preheat the oven to 350°F. Line an 8 × 4-inch loaf pan with parchment paper.

2. **PREPARE THE BROWNIE LAYER:** Microwave the chocolate chips and butter in a microwave-safe bowl on high for 30 seconds; remove and stir. Return to the microwave if not thoroughly melted, and microwave in 15-second intervals until smooth and creamy. (Do not overheat or the chocolate will scorch.)

3. Mix the eggs, vanilla, and sugar in a separate bowl. Stir the egg mixture into the melted chocolate mixture. Add the flour, baking powder, salt, and cocoa, and combine well.

4. Pour the brownie batter into the prepared pan, using an offset spatula to spread the batter evenly. Tap the pan once to remove air bubbles. Bake the brownie layer for 10 minutes, just until the batter looks set. Remove from oven and let cool.

5. **PREPARE THE VANILLA-BEAN CAKE LAYER:** Whisk together the flour, baking powder, baking soda, and salt in a bowl. Combine the sugar and vanilla bean seeds in a food processor and pulse for 30 seconds. Use an electric mixer on medium speed to beat the butter and vanilla-sugar mixture until light and fluffy; beat in the egg. Reduce the speed to low and add half of the flour mixture, beating just to combine. Mix in the buttermilk, then finish with remaining flour mixture.

6. Layer the vanilla-bean cake batter over the baked brownie layer; smooth the top with an offset spatula. Bake for 45 minutes, rotating the pan halfway through, until a toothpick inserted into the center comes out with a few crumbs attached and the cake springs back to the touch.

7. Cool in the pan on a wire rack for 10 minutes. Remove the cake from the pan carefully and cool completely on the wire rack. Slice and serve.

white chocolate mousse

YIELD	4 servings
PREP	15 minutes

2 cups (12 ounces) white chocolate chips

1¾ cups (14 ounces) heavy cream

Fresh strawberries or raspberries, for garnish

*M*ousse, which means "foam" in French, made its debut in the eighteenth century. The high-speed whipping (I can't imagine making this without an electric mixer!) creates air bubbles, giving this marvel its frothy texture.

This two-ingredient dessert is sinfully delicious and can be whipped up in no time. And unlike dark chocolate, white chocolate only contains trace amounts of caffeine so you can indulge and still get a good night's sleep.

1. Heat ¾ cup (6 ounces) of the heavy cream in a saucepan, just until warmed through and bubbles start to appear around the edges. (Do not allow the cream to come to a boil or it will scald.) Remove the cream from the heat and add the white chocolate chips, stirring until the chocolate is completely melted and the mixture is smooth. Set aside to cool.

2. Pour the remaining cup of cream (8 ounces) into a bowl; using an electric mixer on high speed, whip until peaks form. Use a spatula to fold the whipped cream into the cooled white chocolate mixture gradually, until thoroughly blended.

3. Divide the white chocolate mousse among serving dishes. Garnish with the strawberries or raspberries.

mint chocolate mousse

YIELD   6 servings

PREP   5 to 10 minutes

SPECIAL EQUIPMENT

       Parfait or martini glasses

1 cup (6 ounces) bittersweet chocolate chips

1½ cups heavy cream

½ teaspoon pure peppermint extract

Fresh mint sprigs, for garnish, optional

his is my go-to recipe when I need a dessert that achieves maximum impact for minimal effort. Bittersweet chocolate does not contain milk, making it the very best partner for heavy cream. The idea that opposites attract is, I think, why this light and dark, bitter and sweet duo results in such a glorious synthesis of flavor and color. The mint leaf on top suggests there might be a secret ingredient inside. Serve this when you want to surprise and delight your guests.

1. Microwave the chocolate chips in a microwave-safe bowl on high for 30 seconds; remove and stir. Return to the microwave if not thoroughly melted, and microwave in 15-second intervals until smooth and creamy. (Do not overheat or the chocolate will scorch.) Set aside to cool.

2. Pour the cream into a bowl and, using an electric mixer, mix on high speed until peaks form.

3. Blend 2 tablespoons of the cooled chocolate into the whipped cream. Use a spatula to fold the remaining chocolate into the whipped cream gradually, until thoroughly mixed. Stir in the peppermint extract.

4. Divide the mint chocolate mousse among six parfait or martini glasses. Garnish each serving with a sprig of mint, if you choose.

raspberry brownie trifle

YIELD 12 servings

PREP 25 minutes

BAKE 30 minutes

SPECIAL EQUIPMENT
9-inch trifle bowl or 6-ounce parfait glasses

Signature Brownie recipe for
9 × 13-inch pan (page 19)

1½ cups heavy cream

1 cup (6 ounces) semisweet chocolate chips

2 cups fresh raspberries

1 cup (6 ounces) mini semisweet chocolate chips

rifle comes from the Middle English truffle, *and means "fraud, joke, trick"—something inconsequential. That's because centuries ago, desserts were often made using leftovers, and a trifle was a clever way to disguise days-old pound cake.*

Of course, this recipe replaces stale cake with a fresh batch of my Signature Brownies. The alternating layers of chocolate, whipped cream, and raspberries create a simply gorgeous presentation as well as different taste sensations at every level. You can use a traditional 9-inch trifle bowl or individual parfait glasses as shown here. I'm certain your guests will agree this trifle is festive, delicious—and anything but inconsequential.

1. Preheat the oven to 350°F. Grease a 9 × 13-inch pan with butter or nonstick cooking spray; set aside.

2. Prepare the signature brownie recipe and spread the batter in the prepared pan. Bake for 30 minutes, until edges are crisp and the center is completely flat with a crackly surface, and set aside to cool.

3. Pour the cream into a bowl and, using an electric mixer, beat on high speed until peaks form. Set aside.

4. Microwave the semisweet chocolate chips in a microwave-safe bowl on high for 30 seconds; remove and stir. If not thoroughly melted, return to the microwave and microwave in 15-second intervals until smooth.

5. Allow the melted chocolate to cool slightly, and then use a spatula to fold it into the whipped cream until thoroughly blended.

6. Cut the cooled brownies into 1-inch cubes.

7. Place a layer of brownie pieces in the bottom of a 9-inch trifle bowl or individual parfait glasses. Add half of the chocolate whipped cream to the trifle bowl, or distribute it among the parfait glasses, spreading it evenly. Sprinkle half of the berries and half of the mini semisweet chocolate chips. Add another layer of brownie pieces, and then the remaining chocolate whipped cream, spreading it evenly. Sprinkle the top of the trifles with the remaining berries and chocolate chips. Chill for 1 hour and up to 2 days before serving.

brownie soufflés

YIELD 6 servings

PREP 20 minutes

BAKE 25 minutes

SPECIAL EQUIPMENT
6 (4-ounce) ramekins

6 tablespoons salted butter

1 cup (6 ounces) semisweet chocolate chips

¾ cup sugar, plus more for coating ramekins

3 large eggs

2 teaspoons rum

1 teaspoon pure vanilla extract

¾ cup all-purpose flour

½ tablespoon baking soda

hese individual Brownie Soufflés make such a grand presentation. They're rich in color, light as a cloud, and heaven scent. The first spoonful is like a puff of love, a breath of fresh, warm, chocolatey air. Remember, with soufflés, timing is everything, so don't open the oven until the timer beeps, and make sure your guests are ready to dive in as soon as they're served.

1. Preheat the oven to 350°F. Grease 6 ramekins with nonstick cooking spray and sprinkle each ramekin with sugar to coat.

2. Microwave the chocolate chips and butter in a microwave-safe bowl on high for 30 seconds; remove and stir. Return to the microwave if not thoroughly melted, and microwave in 15-second intervals until smooth and creamy. (Do not overheat or the chocolate will scald.) Set aside to cool.

3. Use an electric mixer to mix the eggs and sugar in a separate bowl for 3 to 4 minutes until fluffy. Stir in the rum and vanilla. Add a small amount of the egg mixture to the melted chocolate and mix. Use a spatula to fold the remaining egg mixture into the chocolate and blend thoroughly. Mix together the flour and baking soda in a separate bowl and gradually add the flour mixture to the chocolate and egg mixture until thoroughly combined.

4. Pour ½ cup of the soufflé mixture into each ramekin. Put the ramekins on a baking sheet and bake for 25 minutes, until batter rises slightly above rim of dish and edges appear crisp. Serve warm.

brownies flambé

YIELD	12 servings
PREP	25 minutes
BAKE	30 minutes
SPECIAL EQUIPMENT	
	Extra-large scoop; culinary torch

Signature Brownie recipe for
9 × 13-inch pan (page 19)

MERINGUE

6 egg whites

¼ teaspoon cream of tartar

⅓ cup sugar

1½ cups brandy

Meringue is for pies, right? I mean whoever heard of putting whipped egg whites on brownies? Well, one Fourth of July, I had just taken a pan of brownies out of the oven when I had this bright idea: We could have our own mini fireworks after dinner! All I had to do was pile a mountain of meringue on individual brownies, add brandy, light a match, and, ta-da, everyone would have his or her own sparkling dessert. The white of the meringue under the red and blue flame twinkled our country's colors for just a moment. To my surprise, everyone started clapping. Serve this when you want to impress your guests. And, for maximum effect, be sure to dim the lights.

1. Preheat the oven to 350°F. Grease a 9 × 13-inch pan with nonstick cooking spray and set aside.

2. Prepare the signature brownie recipe according to instructions. Pour the batter into the prepared pan and bake for 30 minutes, until edges are crisp and the center is completely flat with a crackly surface. Set aside to cool.

3. **PREPARE THE MERINGUE:** Whip the egg whites with an electric mixer on high until frothy. Add the cream of tartar and continue beating until stiff peaks form. Add the sugar gradually, and continue to beat until thoroughly blended.

4. Cut the brownies into 12 bars and place them on individual serving dishes. Use an extra-large scoop to measure portions of the meringue on top of each brownie.

5. Use a culinary torch to scorch the top and sides of each meringue. Pour 2 tablespoons of brandy over each meringue, light the brandy with a match for the presentation, and serve immediately.

lava cakes

YIELD 6 servings

PREP 15 minutes

BAKE 10 to 12 minutes

SPECIAL EQUIPMENT

6 custard cups

6 tablespoons salted butter, softened and cut into small pieces

⅓ cup all-purpose flour, plus more for dusting

6 large eggs

⅓ cup granulated sugar plus 3 teaspoons for the ramekins

1½ teaspoons pure vanilla extract

½ teaspoon salt

2 cups (12 ounces) semisweet chocolate chips

Ice cream or confectioners' sugar, for serving

I f only real volcanoes spewed melted chocolate instead of molten lava, the world would be a much happier place. For those who've never eaten a lava cake, mere words cannot describe the experience. It deserves a string of exclamations in all caps: OH MY WARM, RICH, OOEY-GOOEY CHOCOLATE—WOW! And only ice cream or confectioners' sugar is worthy of sharing the same plate—along with a raspberry or two. Save this dessert for special occasions and serve with chilled flutes of champagne.

1. Preheat the oven to 425°F. Grease 6 custard cups with butter, dust them with flour, and set aside.

2. Use an electric mixer to beat together the butter, eggs, ⅓ cup of the sugar, and the vanilla on medium speed until thoroughly combined. Add the flour and salt and continue mixing for 1 minute.

3. Microwave the chocolate chips in a microwave-safe bowl on high for 30 seconds; remove and stir. Return to the microwave if not thoroughly melted, and microwave in 15-second intervals until smooth and creamy. (Do not overheat or the chocolate will scorch.) Allow to cool slightly, and then add a small amount of the melted chocolate to the butter and flour mixture, mixing to combine. Add the rest of the melted chocolate gradually, mixing on low speed until thoroughly blended.

4. Sprinkle each prepared custard cup with ½ teaspoon sugar. Swirl to cover the bottom and sides so the cakes will release easily from the cups.

5. Fill each custard cup three-quarters full with the batter and put them on a baking sheet. Bake for 10 to 12 minutes, until the edges pull away from the sides of the cups.

6. Allow to cool for 2 to 3 minutes, then invert the cups to release each lava cake on a serving dish. Top each cake with a scoop of ice cream, or sprinkle with confectioners' sugar.

bananas foster blondie parfait

YIELD   12 servings

PREP   35 minutes

BAKE   25 minutes (do not overbake)

SPECIAL EQUIPMENT

12 parfait glasses

Blonde Brownie recipe (page 20);
no additional chips

BANANAS FOSTER MIXTURE

8 tablespoons (1 stick) salted butter

1 cup dark brown sugar, packed

2 tablespoons dark rum

¾ cup heavy cream

1 teaspoon pure vanilla extract

6 ripe bananas, sliced

¾ cup walnuts, chopped

This parfait is an absolutely delicious fusion of Bs: bananas, brown sugar, butter. It's my take on the bananas Foster recipe made famous by Brennan's in New Orleans. Now, New Orleans was, and still is, a port of call for ships carrying bananas from Central and South America. In the 1950s, Mr. Brennan asked his chef to create a recipe to take advantage of the fruit's year-round availability. Today, at Brennan's, it takes about 35,000 pounds of bananas to fill the annual demand for this yummy dessert. (The "B" I add to the mix is brownies, of course.)

1. Preheat the oven to 350°F. Grease or spray a 9 × 13-inch pan and set aside.

2. Prepare the blonde brownie recipe according to directions. Pour the batter into the prepared pan and bake for 25 minutes, until toothpick inserted in center comes out clean. Set aside to cool.

3. PREPARE THE BANANAS FOSTER MIXTURE: Melt the butter in a medium saucepan, stir in the brown sugar until well blended, and bring to a simmer. Stir in the rum, cream, and vanilla gradually until blended. Add the sliced bananas and walnuts to the pan and continue cooking until the mixture returns to a simmer. Remove from the heat and set aside to cool slightly.

4. ASSEMBLE THE PARFAITS: Remove the blonde brownies from the pan. Trim away the crisp edges and cut the brownie into quarters. Put the brownies in a food processor and mix for 1 minute, or until the mixture is easy to scoop out into portions.

5. Scoop 2 tablespoons of the blonde brownie mixture into the bottom of each parfait glass. Add a layer of the bananas Foster mixture, then another layer of blonde brownies. Top each glass with the bananas Foster mixture. Chill until ready to serve.

"brownie-fied" strawberries

YIELD   12 strawberries

PREP   15 to 20 minutes

SPECIAL EQUIPMENT

Piping bag with swirl tip;
¾-ounce fluted paper cups

½ cup Brownie Filling (recipe, page 43)

1 dozen fresh large strawberries

*C*hocolate-covered strawberries are stunning, but there's simply no mystery to them. You know what's underneath the chocolate, right? A strawberry. No surprise there. Now, imagine if you sneaked a bit of chocolate into the center of the strawberry—and not just any chocolate—but rich brownie chocolate. Wouldn't that be a switch worthy of your next dinner party?

1. Wash the strawberries and pat dry. Remove the stems and scoop out the centers with a paring knife.

2. Prepare the brownie filling according to instructions. (Store any leftovers in the refrigerator in an airtight container for up to one month.)

3. Pipe 1 teaspoon of brownie filling into the center of each strawberry.

4. Place each strawberry in a fluted paper cup and serve.

brownie
fun

three of these recipes serve a crowd and taste just like popular candy bars; one uses a slow cooker (I know—who knew that would work?!); and two others provide a single serving of chocolate brownie heaven. Go ahead, have some. Fun, that is.

chocolate brittled surprise bars

YIELD	24 bars
PREP	20 minutes
BAKE	8 minutes

M y husband, Harry, likes baked goods, but he L-O-V-E-S candy bars. So I dreamed up this recipe just for him. (He says they remind him of his favorite Butterfinger® bars.) And surprise, surprise, they're now his absolute favorite sweet to snack on. And that's saying something, since he pretty much sampled every dessert I made during the creation of this cookbook!

BROWNIE BRITTLE™ CRUST

8 tablespoons (1 stick) salted butter, melted

2 cups BROWNIE BRITTLE™ (one 5-ounce bag = 1 cup crushed) or chocolate wafers crushed in a food processor

PEANUT BUTTERY CANDY FILLING

2¼ cups candy corn

1½ cups creamy peanut butter (all-natural recommended)

SEMISWEET CHOCOLATE TOPPING

1½ cups (9 ounces) semisweet chocolate chips

¾ teaspoon vegetable shortening or coconut oil

1. Preheat the oven to 350°F. Grease a 9 × 13-inch pan with butter or nonstick cooking spray and set aside.

2. **PREPARE THE BROWNIE BRITTLE™ CRUST:** Mix the butter and crushed BROWNIE BRITTLE™ until thoroughly combined. Press the mixture firmly and evenly into the bottom of the prepared pan. Bake for 8 minutes, and then set aside to cool.

3. **PREPARE THE PEANUT BUTTERY CANDY FILLING:** Melt the candy corn in a double boiler or microwave it in a microwave-safe bowl for 30 seconds; remove and stir. Continue microwaving in 15-second intervals until smooth. (Do not overheat.) Add the peanut butter and mix until thoroughly combined. Scoop the filling onto the cooled crust, spreading it evenly.

4. **PREPARE THE SEMISWEET CHOCOLATE TOPPING:** Microwave the chocolate chips and shortening in a microwave-safe bowl on high for 30 seconds; remove and stir. Return to the microwave if not thoroughly melted, and microwave in 15-second intervals until smooth and creamy. (Do not overheat or the chocolate will scorch.)

5. Spread the melted chocolate over the peanut buttery filling and chill in the refrigerator just until set, about 15 to 20 minutes.

6. Return to room temperature before cutting into 24 bars and serving.

Butterfinger® is a registered trademark of Societé des Produits Nestlé S.A.

slow-cooker fudge brownies

YIELD 6 servings

PREP 15 minutes

COOK 2 to 3 hours

SPECIAL EQUIPMENT

4 ½- to 6-quart slow cooker

Signature Brownie recipe for an 8 × 8-inch pan (page 19)

1 package (3.4 ounces) instant chocolate pudding mix

2 cups milk

Vanilla ice cream or whipped cream, for serving

Semisweet chocolate chips, for garnish, optional

Next time it's your turn to host book club, whip up a batch of these. Plug in the slow cooker about half an hour before your friends arrive. Imagine their delight when they're greeted by the scent of warm chocolate—for the next couple hours. What could you possibly be making that smells so good yet requires no attention?

You'll solve the mystery of what's for dessert once you lift the lid off your slow cooker. This gooey, fudgy infusion of chocolate, topped with ice cream or a dollop of whipped cream, is guaranteed to receive rave reviews—and provide a satisfying ending to a fun evening.

1. Grease a slow-cooker pot with nonstick cooking spray and set the temperature on high.

2. Prepare the signature brownie batter and set aside.

3. Pour the pudding mix into a bowl, add the milk, and use an electric mixer to mix thoroughly, beating for 2 minutes or as directed on the package.

4. Pour the brownie batter into the preheated slow cooker, then pour the pudding mixture over the batter. Place a paper towel under the lid to absorb any condensation and bake the brownie mixture on high for 2 to 3 hours until the edges are set and the center is still moist.

5. Scoop the warm fudge mixture into dessert bowls. Top each serving with your choice of ice cream or whipped cream, and sprinkle with chocolate chips, if desired.

dirt cups

YIELD   4 servings

PREP   20 minutes

1 cup (6 ounces) semisweet
chocolate chips

1½ cups heavy cream

2 cups BROWNIE BRITTLE™
(one 5-ounce bag = 1 cup crushed)
or chocolate wafers crushed in
a food processor

8 tablespoons (1 stick) salted
butter, melted

Gummy worms, for garnish

*W*hat a grubby name for such a scrumptious treat. That silly camp song,
"Nobody likes me, Everybody hates me, Guess I'll go eat worms…" inspired
me to garnish my brownie Dirt Cups with gummy worms. Trust me. Serve these and
everybody will like you, really like you—especially the kids!*

1. Melt the chocolate chips in microwave-safe bowl on high for 30 seconds;
   remove and stir. Return to the microwave and heat in 15-second intervals
   until smooth. Set aside to cool.

2. Mix the crushed BROWNIE BRITTLE™ with the melted butter and set
   aside.

3. Use an electric mixer on high speed to beat the cream until soft peaks form.
   Add a small amount of the cooled melted chocolate to the whipped cream
   and, using a spatula, gently fold it in. Add the rest of the melted chocolate
   gradually, folding it in with the spatula.

4. Place a large scoop of the chocolate whipped cream mixture into the
   bottom of 4 (6-ounce) glasses and cover with a layer of the BROWNIE
   BRITTLE™ crumbles, dividing them evenly. Garnish with the gummy
   worms and serve.

brownie in a mug

YIELD	1 mugful
PREP	5 minutes
BAKE	1½ minutes

¼ cup sugar

¼ cup all-purpose flour

2 tablespoons 100% baking cocoa

3 tablespoons water

2 tablespoons salted butter, melted

¼ teaspoon pure vanilla extract

2 tablespoons semisweet chocolate chips

*B*ored with ice cream? No time to bake? Still want something sweet to eat? How about a mugful of brownie? This eggless wonder can be whipped up just about as quick as you can scoop ice cream into a bowl. The difference is it's warm and fudgy and made to order. Clean up's a piece of cake, too. Simply plop your mug and fork in the dishwasher.

1. Combine the sugar, flour, and cocoa in a large mug and whisk together with a fork. Add the water, melted butter, and vanilla and mix thoroughly to incorporate. Stir in the chocolate chips to evenly distribute.

2. Place the mug in a microwave on a microwave-safe dish and microwave on high for 1½ minutes, until a light crust forms on the surface. Grab a spoon!

"haute" chocolate

3 tablespoons Brownie Filling
(recipe, page 43)

1¼ cups milk

Whipped cream, optional

I call this "Haute" Chocolate because the taste is "fashionably elegant." But, trust me, the recipe is down to earth, and oh-so-simple: It uses Brownie Filling left over from one of my other recipes. No filling left over? You can whip up another batch in a jiffy.

Warm the brownie filling and ¼ cup milk in a small saucepan over medium heat and stir until blended. Pour in the remaining 1 cup milk and whisk until heated through. Garnish with whip cream, if desired.

friendship brownies

YIELD   9 to 12 brownies

PREP   15 minutes

BAKE   30 minutes

SPECIAL EQUIPMENT

Quart-size glass jar with a
tight-fitting lid

DRY BROWNIE MIX

1¼ cups all-purpose flour

1¾ cups sugar

¼ teaspoon salt

½ teaspoon baking powder

¾ cup 100% baking cocoa

1 cup (6 ounces) semisweet
chocolate chips

**ADDITIONAL INGREDIENTS TO
FINISH THE BROWNIES**

12 tablespoons (1½ sticks) salted
butter, melted

2 large eggs, beaten

2 teaspoons pure vanilla extract

1 tablespoon water

Have a special friend with a sweet tooth? This brownie starter kit makes a fun and thoughtful gift—especially during the holidays. It's also a loving way to send a little taste of home to a son or daughter who's away at school.

Simply mix the dry ingredients together and put into a quart-size mason jar or other glass container with a tight-fitting lid. FYI: Mason jars come in different colors so pick one that matches your pal's kitchen. Remember to send along the instructions for mixing and baking the brownies.

Be a friend to yourself as well. If you enjoy entertaining, this recipe allows you to get a jumpstart on dessert. You can mix the dry ingredients days ahead of time. Then all you have to do on the day of your party is add the wet ingredients and bake.

1. Put the flour in a 1-quart glass jar with a lid. Add the sugar, salt, and baking powder, and then the cocoa in layers. Top with the chocolate chips.

2. Cover and store, or give as a gift, accompanied by the instructions (opposite) on a recipe card.

> Want to make this an extra special gift? Use a decorative canister to hold the dry ingredients and to eventually store the homemade brownies in. If the canister lid doesn't fit tightly, seal the dry ingredients in a plastic bag and place it inside the canister along with the directions.

friendship brownie mix

1. Preheat the oven to 350°F.

2. Grease an 8 × 8-inch pan with butter or nonstick cooking spray and set aside.

3. Melt 12 tablespoons (1½ sticks) salted butter. Add 2 beaten eggs, 2 teaspoons pure vanilla extract, and 1 tablespoon water and mix well.

4. Pour the egg mixture into a large bowl.

5. Use a spatula to mix in the dry brownie mix gradually until thoroughly combined.

6. Pour into the prepared pan and bake for 30 minutes, until edges are crisp and the center is completely flat with a crackly surface.

7. Cool completely, and then cut into squares or bars.

index

acknowledgments

To Adam Cohen, who set me on the cookbook path by "schlepping" me all over NYC to meet with book agents. I thought he was crazy to think there would be any interest in me, but by the end of the day we had offers from all three of the agents we met with.

To Dee Moustakas for her talent and patience. Dee and I have a 30-year professional relationship and friendship. She gets inside my head and finishes my sentences. It doesn't get any better than that.

To Barbara Riley, whom I met a year after Dee. We were (and still are) the three amigos. Barb quarterbacked this project and did an amazing job keeping us all on track.

To Jerry Bello. Without Jerry, there would be no cookbook, because no one would have ever heard of Sheila G or BROWNIE BRITTLE™. Jerry and I met in December 2011, and he knew at once that BROWNIE BRITTLE™ was special. He not only invested in the brand, he invested in me. He gave BROWNIE BRITTLE™ a personality by insisting that we put my picture and story on the bag. And then he catapulted it into the marketplace. We went from 200,000 bags on store shelves in 2011 to over 25 MILLION bags on store shelves three years later. There are no words to express my profound gratitude.

To Sarah Passick and Celeste Fine, my agents at Stirling Lord. This cookbook was just as much your vision as mine. Thank you for believing in me and supporting me all the way.

To publisher Kyle Cathie, my editor Jessica Goodman, publicist Ron Longe, and the entire creative team: photographer Tina Rupp, food stylist Lisa Homa, prop stylist Karin Olsen, and designer Alison Lew. Thank you for your insight, guidance, and talent.

To my husband, Harry B. Mains, who never complained about staying home evenings and weekends for weeks at a time, so I could stay on schedule with this cookbook, and all the while, reminding me how proud he is of me.

To my mother Hilda Diamond and my grandmother Rose Siegel, whose passion for baking was contagious. They instilled in me two important lessons that have lasted a lifetime: If you're going to indulge, make sure it's worth it. And home baked is always worth it. As a result, I've never felt a bit of guilt when biting into a velvety cheesecake or the perfect chocolate chip cookie.

To my dad and role model Marty Diamond. He taught me the importance of following your passion and doing what you love.

To Rachael Quintana and Devin Kaminski, my two wonderful children, who have cheered me on every step of the way. When I look back at the challenges I overcame and the sacrifices I made over the years, I realize how much of it was driven by my love and commitment to you and my intense desire to set the best example possible.

To Judi Torres, my sister and my first best friend. Her unconditional love is a gift I've cherished my entire life. Whether the situation calls for a sword and a shield or a pair of pompoms, she is always, always there for me!

To Martha Aronson, my best friend, confidante, and soul sister. I'm pretty sure God put her in my path because He knew I was going to need someone to pick me up, cheer me on, kick me in the butt, provide some sage advice—and every once in a while, offer a shoulder to cry on. In good times and bad, it's Martha, me, and a chilled bottle of chardonnay.